John Paul II in the Holy Land:
In His Own Words

Studies in Judaism and Christianity

Exploration of Issues in the Contemporary Dialogue Between Christians and Jews

Editor in Chief for
Stimulus Books
Helga Croner

Editors
Lawrence Boadt, CSP
Helga Croner
Rabbi Leon Klenicki
Kevin A. Lynch, CSP
Dennis McManus
Dr. Ann Riggs
Rabbi Leonard Schoolman

 A STIMULUS BOOK

John Paul II in the Holy Land: In His Own Words

*with Christian and Jewish Perspectives
by Yehezkel Landau and
Michael McGarry, CSP*

edited by Lawrence Boadt, CSP
and Kevin di Camillo

A STIMULUS BOOK

PAULIST PRESS ◆ NEW YORK ◆ MAHWAH, N.J.

Library of Congress Cataloging-in-Publication Data

Landau, Yehezkel.
    John Paul II in the Holy Land : In his own words : with Christian and Jewish perspectives by Yehezkel Landau and Michael McGarry. Edited by Lawrence Boadt and Kevin di Camillo.
       p. cm. — (Studies in Judaism and Christianity) (Exploration of issues in the contemporary dialogue between Christians and Jews)
    "A Stimulus book."
    Includes bibliographical references.
    ISBN 0-8091-4317-8 (alk. paper)
    1. John Paul II, Pope, 1920—Travel—Palestine. 2. Palestine—Description and travel. 3. Palestine in Christianity. 4. Catholic Church—Relations—Judaism. 5. Judaism—Relations—Catholic Church. I. McGarry, Michael. B. II. Title. III. Series. IV. Series: Exploration of issues in the contemporary dialogue between Christians and Jews.

BX1378.5.L36 2005
282'.5694—dc22

                                   2004026803

Published by Paulist Press
997 Macarthur Boulevard
Mahwah, New Jersey 07430

www.paulistpress.com

Printed and bound in the United States of America

Contents

CONTENTS

Contents

Publisher's Introduction

Lawrence Boadt, CSP

*I*n his quarter century as pope, John Paul II has done more for establishing the importance of Catholic dialogue with the Jewish people than all the efforts during the two millennia before him. Not only did he reach out to former Jewish friends and acquaintances who had, like himself, survived the Nazi terror in Poland during World War II, but he established bonds with the chief rabbi of Rome, set in motion the first diplomatic recognition of the State of Israel by the Vatican, and made a public expression of regret in the name of the whole Catholic Church for injustice to Jews—an important theme of his pastoral leadership. His visit to the Middle East in March 2000 was a moving and extraordinarily rich experience, a high point for him both personally and as the leader of the Catholic Church. As he had said so often, it was his dream fulfilled that he could, as "the servant of the servants of God," walk in the land and visit the places where Jesus had lived and walked.

This book chronicles that visit by following his itinerary and providing his profound reflections at each stop on his journey. It was truly a *pilgrimage* of faith for him in which he would bring home a renewed and strengthened conviction of the value of the dialogue that he had worked so hard to foster between Jews and Christians, and a greater trust that God was indeed the one at work in building this new spirit.

Besides the pope's own words, we are very pleased to present the reflections of two scholars and active participants in building that dialogue from the ground up. One is a Jew and one is a Catholic. One is a Hebrew scholar and one is a priest. Both have endured the trials and hardships of doing dialogue in the Holy Land itself, bridging the passions and the differences between Christians and Jews and Muslims, and showing respect and patience and commitment to all sides. Both know firsthand the pain and the joy each individual faces who enters into dialogue in the troubled motherland of our mutual faiths.

Father Michael McGarry, CSP, is the rector of the Tantur Ecumenical Institute, which sits astride the dividing line between West Bank Bethlehem and the city of Jerusalem. He has worked tirelessly for six years to build the bridges of understanding among the Jews, Muslims, and Christians in one of the tensest hotspots of the Holy Land. He is also a well-known writer and thinker on the question of Jewish-Christian dialogue.

Professor Yehezkel Landau was the cofounder and director of the Open House Center for Jewish-Arab Coexistence in Ramle, Israel, from 1991 to 2003, and director of the Oz veShalom-Netivot Shalom Religious Zionist Peace Movement in the previous decade, and so struggled for understanding and peace in the most difficult of circumstances. Professor Landau is now a faculty associate in interfaith relations at the Hartford Seminary.

The collective reflections of Professor Landau and Father McGarry situate for both Catholics and Jews the importance of the pope's visit to this most sacred land, and they candidly explore the difficulties that, regrettably, still remain.

The pope has been the undisputed leader in fostering Jewish-Christian dialogue for over twenty-five years. He has labored intensely to change the hearts and minds of both sides to learn to listen and trust one another, and he has courageously expressed, on behalf of the Church, regret for the sins of Christians against the Jews over the centuries. His visit to the very heart of the geography sacred to the three most populous monotheistic faiths marked a high point for him that he shared in his heart-moving talks. In this volume, then, we present the speeches he gave on this journey, together with the penetrating insights of Father McGarry and Professor Landau, as a beginning point for all of us to think more seriously on the mystery of God's plans for humankind that are revealed in these two great religions and to learn to listen to one another, trust one another, and love one another more deeply.

TOTUS TUUS
The coat of arms of Johannes Paulus II,
Bishop of Rome

ITINERARY:

Pope John Paul II's Pilgrimage to the Holy Land in the Jubilee Year 2000

DAYS ONE AND TWO: Jordan, March 20–21

1. Arrives in Amman, meets dignitaries
2. Meets with King Abdullah II
3. Mass at Amman Stadium
4. Visits traditional site of Moses' grave
5. Visits the Jordanian site of Jesus' baptism

DAY TWO: Tel Aviv, March 21

1. Arrives at Ben Gurion Airport, meets dignitaries
2. Helicopter to Papal Nuncio's residence in East Jerusalem

DAY THREE: Bethlehem and Dheisheh, March 22

1. Mass at the Church of the Nativity, Manger Square
2. Visits the Cave of the Nativity
3. Visits refugee camp, Dheisheh
4. Meets with Yasser Arafat

DAY FOUR: Jerusalem and Yad Vashem, March 23

1. Mass at the Jerusalem Cenacle
   (the Upper Room of the Last Supper)
2. Meets with the Ashkenazi Chief Rabbi
3. Visits Israeli president Ezer Weizman at his residence
   in West Jerusalem
4. At Yad Vashem, meets with survivors of the *Shoah*
5. At Notre Dame Pontifical Institute, meets
   with chief rabbi and a Muslim judge

DAY FIVE: Galilee, March 24

1. At Korazim, the Mount of the Beatitudes, the only
   outdoor Mass (50,000 in attendance)
2. Private visits to
   — Church of the Multiplication of the Loaves at
     Tabgha
   — Church of the Primacy of Saint Peter at Tabgha
   — Shrine of the House of Saint Peter in Capernaum
3. That evening, returns by helicopter to Papal Nuncio's
   residence in East Jerusalem

DAY SIX: Nazareth, March 25

1. Private prayer at the site of the Annunciation
2. Mass at the Franciscan Basilica of the Annunciation
3. Meets with consuls general of the
   apostolic delegation in Jerusalem

4. Private visit to the Church of All Nations
   in Kidron Valley, the traditional site of Jesus' agony
   in the garden

5. Meets with Greek Orthodox Patriarch of Jerusalem at
   his residence in the "Old City" of Jerusalem

DAY SEVEN: Final Day in Jerusalem, March 26

1. Meets with Grand Mufti Sabri in Mosque Square
   ("Temple Mount")

2. Meets with Rabbi Melchior at the Western Wall
   ("Wailing Wall") where he places prayer
   for forgiveness in the Wall

3. Prays at the Stone of the Anointing

4. Final Mass of his trip at the Basilica
   of the Holy Sepulcher ("Church of the Resurrection")

5. Lunch with the Latin Patriarch, Armenian Patriarch,
   and other Church leaders

6. Unplanned second, private visit to the Holy
   Sepulcher's Chapel of Calvary

The Journey...

Michael McGarry, CSP

It is my fervent wish to visit...the Middle East: Lebanon, Jerusalem, and the Holy Land. It would be very significant if in the year 2000 it were possible to visit the places on the road taken by the people of God of the Old Covenant, starting from the places associated with Abraham and Moses, through Egypt and Mount Sinai, as far as Damascus, the city which witnessed the conversion of St. Paul.[1]

He had dreamed of coming here from the earliest years of his pontificate, but many of his advisers and handlers had persistently counseled him against it. The visit was untimely, they insisted. But in the end and for the millennium, he would not be deterred. Pope John Paul II wanted to mark the Jubilee Year with a pilgrimage to the sacred places of salvation history, beginning with those from the Hebrew Scriptures and concluding with those of the Christian covenant. And so it happened over a number of weeks in 1999 and 2000, culminating in the week of intense, prayerful, and solemn visits in the Holy Land: in Jordan, Israel, and Palestine.

---

1. Pope John Paul II, Apostolic Letter, *Tertio Millennio Adveniente, Origins* 24 (November 24, 1994): 408.

Well could it be said of Pope John Paul II's visit to the Holy Land as was said of an earlier pilgrim to the Holy Land, Egeria:

A longing for God set on fire the heart of this most blessed nun Egeria. In the strength of the glorious Lord she fearlessly set out on an immense journey to the other side of the world. Guided by God, she pressed on until after a time she reached what she had longed for, the most holy places of the birth, passion, and resurrection of the Lord.[2]

Recalling the words of St. Augustine, the Second Vatican Council (1963–65) imaged the Church itself as a pilgrim people: "Like a pilgrim in a foreign land, the Church presses forward amid the persecutions of the world and the consolations of God."[3] And Pope John Paul II, as the leader of that Church, has certainly proved himself, through close to two hundred worldwide journeys, to be a pilgrim. It was with such self-understanding that he came to the Holy Land.

Generations of Christian pilgrims to the Holy Land preceded Pope John Paul II. Egeria was perhaps the most famous of these, who in the late fourth century, in her religious fervor, sought to touch the places, to touch the "fringe of his cloak," as it were (Matt 9:20), so that her

---

2. Egeria, quoted by John Wilkinson, *Egeria's Travels* (London: S.P.C.K., 1973), 98.

3. From "Dogmatic Constitution on the Church," Article 8, in *The Documents of Vatican II*, edited by Walter M. Abbott (New York: Herder and Herder/Association Press, 1966), 24.

body could touch what had touched the body of the One who had saved us all. And that is one of a pilgrimage's purposes: to "touch the places"—to see the rocks, the water; smell the smells; feel the winds; and experience the overwhelming constellation of things that surrounded the life of Jesus. The pilgrim's religious impulse echoed the anonymous woman in Mark's Gospel—"If I only touch his cloak, I will be made well" (9:21). And that was Pope John Paul's intention.

However, in contrast to Pope John Paul, Christians, in their comings to the Holy Land, have not always come in peace or reconciliation. At the end of the eleventh century, Pope Urban II urged faithful Christian soldiers of Europe to go to the Holy Land to rescue it from the infidels, from the Moslems. And so the waves of Christian European onslaughts began, often in genuine faith, to resacralize the land made holy by the footsteps of Jesus. But they came to conquer as well and conquer they did. For about a century the Christians retook the Holy Land but not without exacting a bloody price on those who were living here: Moslems, Jews, and in the later crusades, even other—Eastern—Christians.

If one thing was, and is, true of the Middle East, it is that the peoples of this region have long memories. An event of a thousand years ago is as present to many of them as an event last week is to the Westerner. If it happened two centuries ago or one thousand years ago, it might as well have happened last week. Indeed, I remember one example quite vividly. In February, barely a month before Pope John Paul was to land at Tel Aviv's Ben

Gurion Airport, the Elijah School for the Study of the Wisdom in World Religions assembled a panel to discuss the papal visit. It was comprised of the apostolic nuncio (Msgr. Pietro Sambi), the chief rabbi of Haifa, and the leader of the Islamic movement in Israel. When asked about the possibilities and meaning of the papal visit to the Holy Land, the Muslim representative said, almost without qualification, that if the pope did not apologize for the Crusades, there was no purpose for his coming. For the Muslim representative, that event vividly lives in his memory.

Yes, memories are long in this part of the world. And the Holy Father, keenly aware of such sensitivities, knew that those who call this land their home would carefully scrutinize every moment of his trip.

On the Jewish side, anticipation of the pope's visit was, until about four weeks before his arrival, mixed, to say the least. Indeed, many parts of Israeli society were antagonistic to Pope John Paul's coming, for they, too, carry long memories. As Prime Minister Barak said at Yad Vashem, the Shoah memorial, "Your Holiness, mine is a nation that remembers." In the Israeli press, for weeks before the pope arrived, the nightmare of the *Shoah* was reviewed. The horrid history of Christian treatment of Jews was revisited several times with little reference to more recent healings and progress. Some interpreted the visit as part of a larger Christian plan to evangelize the Jews. Others just didn't quite know what to do with such a personage. "Why can't Christianity in general, and the pope in particular, just leave us alone?" some complained.

What kind of security would he require? How would he respect the Sabbath? And on and on.

Until something happened.

I don't know exactly what it was, but about four weeks before the Holy Father's arrival, there was a shift in Israeli media culture, both electronic and print. Many began to realize that the pope's visit was indeed going to take place despite a few strident voices on the margins. Many began to realize that, far from a burden, his visit might be an opportunity for Israel to show itself as a society open to other world religions and in particular to Christianity.

So then the "spin doctors" began their work. "What was the *real* reason for the pope's visit to Israel? What did he *really* want to accomplish?" Such was many reporters' mantra as they sought out in Jerusalem and Tel Aviv all Christians who spoke their own language. Again, as one who was daily engaged in phone and in-person interviews with the world's press, I began to think hard about this question. I spoke with the apostolic nuncio and many other church people in the Holy City. I read carefully the documents that came from the pope's own hand about his trip. And I repeated to reporters that I thought it only fair to understand the pope's visit to the Holy Land in the words with which he himself framed his trip. For the Holy Father, it was to be a *spiritual* journey, a pilgrimage to the primary sites in the Christian understanding of the history of salvation. These, consequently, included sites drawn from the Hebrew Scriptures in the Jewish understanding of their own history with God. The trip would also include sites made holy by the presence of Jesus and later of the apostle Paul. In all my interviews, I additionally insisted that the pope's visit to the Holy Land had to be understood in the larger context of visits to other countries' holy places; otherwise it was to exaggerate and therefore to distort the part of his pilgrimage that included Israel. Even though in 1965, as archbishop of Krakow in Poland, Cardinal Karol Wojtyla had already visited the Holy Land, now, as Pope John Paul II, in the perspective of the 2000th anniversary of the incarnation, he

> had a strong desire to go personally to pray in the most important places which, from the Old to the New Testament, have seen God's interventions, which culminate in the mysteries of the incarnation and of the passion, death and resurrection of Christ. These places [were] already indelibly etched in [his] memory from the time when in 1965 [he had] had the opportunity to visit the Holy Land.[4]

Political difficulties prevented the pope's visiting Ur of the Chaldees in modern-day Iraq. So not long before his trip to the Holy Land, the Holy Father visited Mount Sinai in Egypt.[5] Tradition holds that there God had bestowed

---

4. Pope John Paul II, Letter, "Pilgrimage to Places Linked to the History of Salvation," in *Origins* 29 (1999): 125–28, at 126.

5. Pope John Paul's visits to the holy sites in Greece and Syria were delayed until 2001 for political reasons. Nonetheless, they too marked spiritually powerful moments as he sought forgiveness from the people of Greece for what Christians had done to them through the centuries, mentioning explicitly the sacking of Constantinople in 1204 by the retreating Fifth Crusade.

the Ten Commandments on Moses and the chosen people. It was to Mount Sinai, also called "Horeb," that Moses had led the Hebrews out of Egyptian slavery. Eventually Moses would lead them to the Holy Land, the "land flowing with milk and honey" (Exod 3:8), but he himself would be denied final entry. His reward, nonetheless, would be to gaze on the land from Mount Nebo, located in the contemporary Hashemite Kingdom of Jordan (see Deut 32:49). Where Moses ended his traveling, Pope John Paul II would begin his, anticipating the hope which that site symbolizes:

> [Moses'] gaze from Nebo is the very symbol of hope. From that mountain he could see that God had kept his promises. Once more, however, he had to abandon himself trustingly to the divine omnipotence for the sake of the final accomplishment of the [plan that had been foretold].[6]

Despite the consistently *spiritual* terms within which he wrote about his visit, both in *Tertio Millennio Adveniente* in 1994 and in "Pilgrimage to Places Linked to the History of Salvation" in 1999, Pope John Paul knew that reporters and other commentators would apply their own template to his journey. So hopefully, but realistically, the Holy Father wrote,

> It would be an exclusively religious pilgrimage in its nature and purpose, and I would be saddened if anyone were to attach other meanings to this plan of

---

6. Pope John Paul II, "Pilgrimage to Places," 127.

mine....To go in a spirit of prayer from one place to another, from one city to another, in the area marked especially by God's intervention, helps us not only to live our life as a journey, but also gives us a vivid sense of a God who has gone before us and leads us on, who himself set out on man's path, a God who does not look down on us from on high, but who became our traveling companion.[7]

And so the pope earnestly strove to explain his pilgrimage as one of the spirit. He would touch the places which God had touched, as he traveled the places where Moses and Jesus had traveled. But history is not always so kind to those who wish their intentions to be clear and unequivocally understood. The shadow of three not-so-spiritual events hovered over both the pope's intentions about the Holy Land and his travels there: (1) the history of Jewish-Christian relations, (2) the Israeli-Palestinian conflict, and (3) the ever-painful divisions within the Christian Church, especially that between the Latin Church of the West and the Churches of the East. Try as he might, the Holy Father could not completely avoid these shadows, even for a "spiritual pilgrimage."

In the West, probably the most poignant backdrop for the Holy Father's trip to the Holy Land was the long, blood- and tear-stained history of Jewish-Christian relations. Indeed, the late Father Edward Flannery, eminent chronicler of that history, once wrote, "Those pages of history Jews have committed to memory are the very ones that

---

7. Ibid., 127–28.

have been torn from Christian (and secular) history books."[8] The Holy Father is not unaware of that history. In fact, he has made a new, positive relationship with Judaism and the Jewish people a trademark of his pontificate. Building on the direction begun at the Second Vatican Council, on almost all his journeys Pope John Paul has regularly met with Jewish leaders. He has referred to the *Shoah* as the tragedy of the 20th Century.[9] And on April 13, 1986, he was the first pope to visit the Rome synagogue. On that very special occasion, to be surpassed in visual drama only by his visit to Jerusalem, Pope John Paul asserted that

> the Church of Christ discovers her "bond" with Judaism by "searching into her own mystery" [see *Nostra Aetate*]. The Jewish religion is not "extrinsic" to us, but in a certain way is "intrinsic" to our own religion. With Judaism, therefore, we have a relationship which we do not have with any other religion. You are our dearly beloved brothers and, in a certain way, it could be said that you are our elder brothers....[The] Jews are beloved of God, who has called them with an irrevocable calling.[10]

---

8. Edward A. Flannery, *The Anguish of the Jews: Twenty-Three Centuries of Antisemitism*. Rev. and Updated. (New York: Paulist Press, 1985), 1.

9. E.g., the pope said, "This is still the century of the *Shoah*, the inhuman and ruthless attempt to exterminate European Jewry," in an address to the Jewish community in Australia, November 26, 1986. Qtd. in John Paul II's *Spiritual Pilgrimage: Texts on Jews and Judaism 1979–1995*,edited by Eugene J. Fisher and Rabbi Leon Klenicki (New York: Crossroad, 1996) 82. See also Eugene J. Fisher and Rabbi Leon Klenicki, *In Our Time: The Flowering of Jewish-Catholic Dialogue* (Mahwah, NJ: Paulist Press, 1990).

10. Address by the pope at the synagogue in Rome, April 13, 1986. Qtd. in *Spiritual Pilgrimage*, 63

As the weeks shortened before the pope's arrival, the Israeli press began to pay attention to this pope's record on Jewish-Catholic relations. One has to remember that the Israeli public, mostly religiously nonobservant, were and are woefully ignorant of the dramatic strides that the Catholic and other Western Churches have made in this regard over the last fifty years. The Israeli press began to highlight these significant advances. Secular writers furiously sought out Catholic and other Christian "experts" to help them write their background stories.

This attention to the Catholic Church's efforts at rapprochement with Judaism and the Jewish people dovetailed with another approaching dramatic moment that anticipated the visit to Israel. Worldwide attention turned to St. Peter's Basilica on March 12, 2000. There, less than two weeks before his arrival in Israel, on behalf of the Roman Catholic Church, Pope John Paul sought forgiveness from the Jewish people:

> God of our fathers, you chose Abraham and his descendants to bring your Name to the nations: we are deeply saddened by the behaviour of those who in the course of history have caused these children of yours to suffer, and asking your forgiveness we wish to commit ourselves to genuine brotherhood with the people of the Covenant.[11]

---

11. "Service Requesting Pardon," *Origins* 29 (March 23, 2000): 40:45–48. It should be carefully noted that nowhere does the Holy Father or official organs of the Catholic Church use the word "apology" in its expression of regret for the many sins and acts of violence committed against the Jewish people through the ages. Only the actual perpetrator can apologize

Many in the Israeli press and elsewhere lamented the lack of an explicit apology or any stronger statement than what the Holy Father came up with in that special ceremony at St. Peter's in Rome. But it must be remembered that a fuller text specifically about the Church and the *Shoah*—not without its own controversy to be sure—had already been issued in March 1998. "We Remember" was the document which sought to address the Church and the *Shoah*. Words subsequent to it, however much some quarters in the Church and some parts of the Jewish community wished, would not go beyond it. While it is outside the scope of this essay to reflect on the Church and the *Shoah*, what is most important here is to realize the local Israeli concerns that formed the backdrop of the papal visit: Would the Holy Father go further than that declaration when he was in Israel? We will say more on that below.

In addition to Jewish concerns about Church involvement in, and responsibility for, the *Shoah*, and in addition to the long history of Jewish-Christian relations, was the more particular Jewish concern about the Catholic Church's political relation to the State of Israel. Only as recently as 1994 had the Holy See (the official political designation of the Catholic Church as a State) opened up full diplomatic relations with the State of Israel.[12] Rehashed in the Israeli press was the meeting of January

---

and only the actual victim can accept an apology. The Church has gotten into trouble, rightfully, for notions of collective guilt; it cannot redeem itself by making collective apologies.

12. See "The Vatican-Israel Fundamental Agreement," *Origins* 23, no. 30 (1994): 525–28.

25, 1904, between Theodor Herzl, the father of modern Zionism, and Pope Pius X. To Herzl's request that the Holy Father support the Jewish return to the Holy Land, Pius X is reported to have replied: "We cannot encourage this movement....The Jews have not recognized our Lord, therefore we cannot recognize the Jewish people....And so, if you come to Palestine and settle your people there, we will be ready with churches and priests to baptize all of you."[13] This story was, predictably, repeated frequently as the time for this pope's visit drew near. While partially muted by the 1994 Fundamental Agreement, the document that normalized relations between the Holy See and the State of Israel, this general hostility also provided a backdrop to the Holy Father's visit.

The pope's pilgrimage to the Holy Land was historic, but it was not unprecedented. In 1964, coming in through the Hashemite Kingdom of Jordan, Pope Paul VI had visited the Holy Land. Obviously, since his visit was before the 1967 war, much more of the land was under Jordanian control than today's divide between Israel and the Palestinian West Bank. Then, because the Holy See was still working its way towards full diplomatic relations with Israel, the protocol and language were very carefully chosen. Arab resistance to recognition of the State was balanced against Catholicism's evolving rapprochement with the State and with Judaism and the Jewish people. Indeed, the still-ongoing Second Vatican Council had not

13. Quoted in Sergio I. Minerbi, *The Vatican and Zionism: Conflict in the Holy Land 1895–1925* (New York: Oxford University Press, 1990), 100–101.

yet promulgated its historic declaration on the Church's relation to the Jewish people, which could not be jeopardized by premature language of recognition. Hindsight may yield different historical wishes for that time, but it was a most delicate moment and required the greatest diplomacy so as not to jeopardize the final positive outcome of the Second Vatican Council. However, whatever the reasons, many Israelis were aware that Pope Paul VI had not uttered the word "Israel" while he conducted his Holy Land pilgrimage and so this, too, provided a backdrop to his successor's arrival in the spring of 2000.[14]

The second major shadow over the pope's historic visit to the Holy Land was the effect it would have on the contemporary struggle between Israelis and Palestinians over the future of peace in the region. Indeed, if the long and sad story of Jewish-Christian relations provided the most difficult *historical* backdrop, the Israeli-Palestinian struggle provided the most difficult *contemporary* backdrop.

---

14. See Anthony Kenny, *Catholics, Jews, and the State of Israel* (New York: Paulist Press, 1993). Curiously, Kenny does not mention the pilgrimage of Pope Paul VI. Also, see George Irani, *The Papacy and the Middle East: The Role of the Holy See in the Arab-Israeli Conflict, 1962–1984* (Notre Dame, IN: University of Notre Dame Press, 1986); Thomas Brechenmacher and Hardy Ostry, *Paul VI—Rom und Jerusalem: Konzil, Pilgerfahrt, Dialog der Religionen* (Trier: Paulinus, 2000); and (no author cited) *Pope Paul VI in the Holy Land* (New York: Herder and Herder, 1964). Pope Paul VI's legacy in the Holy Land was the founding of three institutions: Bethlehem University for the education of Christians and other Palestinians so they would not have to leave the Holy Land for higher education; Epheta, a clinic for those with hearing disorders (very prevalent) in Bethlehem, Beit Jala, and Beit Sahour; and the Tantur Ecumenical Institute in Jerusalem, a research center for Christians from all parts of the Christian family.

Long and exacting were the negotiations as to where exactly—and how long—the pope would visit in the occupied territories of the West Bank. Almost using some kind of scorecard, journalists began to count the minutes the pope's itinerary apportioned to each side.

The pope's lengthy and earnest solicitude for the sufferings of the Palestinian people is well known. What is not so well known, at least in many parts of the Western world, is the fact that the vast majority of Christians native to Israel and Palestine are Arabs. Their actual numbers are small: no more than two percent of Israelis are Christian (living mostly in the Galilee) and a little less than two percent of Palestinians (mostly just south of Jerusalem around Bethlehem), but they witness to an unbroken legacy of Jesus' disciples since the first century. Because these local, well-educated Christians are such a small minority, they are apprehensive about their future. Sad to report, they have been emigrating at an alarming rate over the last few decades. This emigration has resulted in thriving Palestinian communities in the United States, Central America, and Chile.[15] A Holy Land without an indigenous Christian community is a tragic and real possibility—a museum of dead stones set as memorials to Jesus of Nazareth. Today the dismal prospects for a more-than-subsistence economy in the West Bank—whenever it becomes a sovereign state— offer little hope.

---

15. It is reported that there are today more Christians born in Bethlehem living in Santiago, Chile, than still living in Bethlehem.

Along with the pope's understandable concern for the Christian community in the Holy Land was his well-known longing for peace in the region and for a diplomatic solution to the complicated problems that must be addressed for such a peace to occur. While his journey was to be a "spiritual pilgrimage," Pope John Paul II could not avoid these political issues. He would have to address the plight of the Palestinians in general and the Christians in particular. This he would do in his visit to Bethlehem, as we shall review below.

Finally, in his visit to the Mother Church, the mother of all churches, Jerusalem, Pope John Paul II would have to address the division of the children of this sorrowful mother. As my Tantur predecessor and Catholic ecumenist Father Thomas Stransky has often said, none of the divisions of the church originated here—they have all been imported. And they are here in depth and abundance.[16]

Western pilgrims are often shocked by these divisions when they visit for the first time the most sacred of Christian sites, the Church of the Holy Sepulcher (or, as

---

16. On March 12, 2000, in the same service mentioned above in which the Holy Father sought the forgiveness from the Jewish people, he prayed, "Merciful Father, on the night before his Passion your Son prayed for the unity of those who believe in him: in disobedience to his will, however, believers have opposed one another, becoming divided, and have mutually condemned one another and fought against one another. We urgently implore your forgiveness and we beseech the gift of a repentant heart, so that all Christians, reconciled with you and with one another will be able, in one body and in one spirit to experience anew the joy of full communion. We ask this through Christ our Lord."

the Eastern Churches more aptly call it, the Church of the Resurrection). There pilgrims see, in undisguised and dramatic expression, the divisions of the Church worked out in centuries-old bickering and fights over centimeters of dust this way, and hours of services that way. Within the one building dwell—in a relationship of sometimes-tense, *status quo* agreements—the Greek Orthodox, Syrian Orthodox, Armenian Orthodox, Coptic Orthodox, and Latin (Roman) Catholic Churches. Relegated to its roof are the long-suffering Ethiopian Orthodox monks. Churches from the breakup of Western Christianity dating from the sixteenth-century Reformation are not represented at all within the building.[17] In his publicly stated intention to visit the Holy Land, His Holiness said,

> In this journey through the places where God chose to pitch his "tent" among us, great is my desire to be welcomed as a pilgrim and brother...by the other churches which have lived uninterruptedly in the holy places and have been their custodians with fidelity and love of the Lord. More than any other pilgrimage which I have made, the one I am about to undertake in the Holy Land during the jubilee event will be marked by the desire expressed in Christ's prayer to the Father that his disciples "may all be one" (John 17:21), a prayer which challenges us more vigorously at the exceptional time which opens the third millennium....I would be happy if we could gather together in the places of our common origin to bear witness to Christ our unity and to

17. They are now symbolically present through the Presbyterian-designed renovated dome inside the church.

confirm our mutual commitment to the restoration of full communion.[18]

In the complicated and tradition-laden world of the Church of the Holy Land, Pope John Paul's desire for drawing together various parts of the Christian family would be a delicate process. About this, more will be said below.

DAY ONE: Jordan and Mount Nebo

After a private retreat in the Vatican—this in lieu of visiting Ur in modern-day Iraq—and after his visit to Mount Sinai in Egypt, the Holy Father looked to his extended time in the Holy Land. He started in the Hashemite Kingdom of Jordan since he wished to follow the path for the entrance into Israel that Moses had taken with his people. Ironically, Moses himself was never to set foot on the land as a punishment for disobeying God in the desert. But before Moses would die, God would allow him to gaze over the land across the Jordan from the site now traditionally associated with that moment: Mount Nebo.

As would become almost ritual during the pope's pilgrimage, the shutters of a hundred cameras clicked as the Holy Father knelt in prayer to read and contemplate the account of the caravan of the chosen people. Indeed, many veteran papal observers remark on this Holy Father's uncanny ability to close out from his view and

18. Pope John Paul II, "Pilgrimage to Places," 128.

attention all outside influences as he goes into an almost trancelike posture of prayer. But he also has the ability to focus keenly on the interchange that may bookend such moments of prayer. After examining the mosaics that adorn a chapel which tradition holds as the place of Moses' grave, Pope John Paul listened intently as Jordanian Catholic school girls, led enthusiastically by a Franciscan sister, sang hymns in both Arabic and Latin.

This scene on Mount Nebo was played out after King Abdullah II had met Pope John Paul II at the airport with the warm and gracious welcome: "It is now your turn that reminds us of important facts lest they be forgotten: the virtues of faith and the absolute need for forgiveness of one's enemies." Pope John Paul II replied as graciously: "In this area of the world there are grave and urgent issues of justice, of the rights of peoples and nations, which have to be resolved for the good of all concerned and as a condition for lasting peace."[19] He went on to praise "the already fruitful Christian-Muslim dialogue which is being conducted in Jordan, particularly through the Royal Interfaith Institute."

The Holy Father showed great pastoral solicitude for the tiny Latin Catholic population of Jordan—about seventy thousand people, or 1 percent of the population—by presiding at an outdoor mass in Amman. As happened at many of his stops, hundreds of children had been scrupu-

19. Here and for the rest of this essay, all quotations from government officials and Pope John Paul II come from the *Bulletin, Associated Christian Press*, No. 412, published by the Christian Information Centre, Jerusalem, June–July–August 2000.

lously rehearsed to sing and, here, to make their first communion. To them he said, "Jesus is your best friend; he knows what is in your hearts. Stay close to him, and in your prayers remember the Church and the pope." In Amman the pope invoked the image of John the Baptist as the one who points the way to salvation, to Jesus Christ. This was in anticipation of his visiting *two* sites for the baptism of the Lord, one on Jordan's side of the Jordan River and one on the Israeli side of the river. (Here, as in many places in the Holy Land, evenhandedness would push some of the historical possibilities.)

DAY TWO: Tel Aviv and Israel

As noted above, Pope John Paul was not the first modern pope to come to the Holy Land. Pope Paul VI had come, via Jordan, in 1964 on a hastily planned trip to underscore his personal faith and to engage in a spiritual pilgrimage. During the weeks anticipating Pope John Paul's arrival, some journalists made much of the fact that Pope Paul had not mentioned the words "State of Israel" during his few hours on the Israeli side of the border. Hindsight and a different historical situation made too much of this omission, however. Pope Paul VI was still working behind the scenes to help move forward the now-famous *Nostra Aetate*, which came to express the beginning of a sea change in Catholic-Jewish relations. Strong opposition to this declaration emanated from some bishops in Arab countries, so the midwifing of this most important document was most delicate.

For this visit, the Holy Father would have the confidence and change of historical situation to refer directly and without nuance to the State of Israel. But even more dramatic than the change of vocabulary was the change of perception. As mentioned above, the 1904 negative encounter between Theodor Herzl and Pope Pius X had been repeated in much of the Israeli press. So with that as a background, the dramatic image of the aged, but still-vigorous pontiff being greeted at Ben Gurion airport by the prime minister and the president of the State of Israel caused for many a shift of paradigms, a culmination of a pontificate committed to new relations between Catholics and Jews. As Israeli journalist Yossi Klein Halevi noted in an article before the Papal visit:

> When Pope John Paul II lands at Ben Gurion Airport..., he will be embodying the Vatican's new theology, whose key point is that the Jews are not rejected but still blessed by God....Indeed, in 2,000 years, no individual has done more to foster reconciliation between Christians and Jews than this Polish pope....Now he will be the first pontiff to come to Israel with the benefit of full diplomatic relations—which he initiated in the 1993 over protests from Vatican diplomats who feared anti-Christian backlash in the Muslim world.[20]

Klein-Halevi's words proved to be true throughout the Holy Father's visit to the Holy Land. When he landed,

---

20. Yossi Klein Halevi, "Pilgrimage into the Lion's Den," *The Jerusalem Report*, March 27, 2000, 16.

however, the Holy Father tried, as before, to frame his visit in spiritual terms:

> My visit is both a personal pilgrimage and the spiritual journey of the Bishop of Rome to the origins of our faith in "the God of Abraham, of Isaac and of Jacob" (Exod 3:15). It is part of a larger pilgrimage of prayer and thanksgiving which led me first to Sinai, the Mountain of the covenant, the place of the decisive revelation which shaped the subsequent history of salvation.

As spiritual as his journey was, however, Pope John Paul acknowledged the State of Israel a number of times in his greetings. And he hoped that his visit would have not only personal consequences for his own faith life, but also social consequences in promoting

> an increase of interreligious dialogue that will lead Jews, Christians and Muslims to seek in their respective beliefs, and in the universal brotherhood that unites all the members of the human family, the motivation and the perseverance to work for the peace and justice which the peoples of the Holy Land do not yet have, and for which they yearn so deeply.

DAY THREE: Bethlehem and Dheisheh

Except for the stop at the two sites of Jesus' baptism at the Jordan, the Holy Father had now arrived in the footsteps of Jesus by visiting the place of his birth, as he put it, "the heart of my Jubilee Pilgrimage." There in Manger Square of Bethlehem—only a few years ago a predominantly Christian town and now about 70 percent Muslim—the Holy Father would preside at the Eucharist for the city's Christians, almost all of whom are Palestinian. Among the locals were also the dozens of international sisters, priests, and lay workers who staff the various schools, clinics, convents, monasteries, and university of the area. On an outdoor altar in front of the Nativity Church—the church longest in continuous use in the world—Pope John Paul would bring the message of the newborn Messiah one more time: "The great mystery of divine self-emptying, the work of our redemption unfolding in weakness: this is no easy truth. The Savior was born in the night in the darkness, in the silence and poverty of the cave of Bethlehem."

Besides the local Christian community and dignitaries, the pope greeted the "Muslim Community of Bethlehem and pray[ed] for a new era of understanding and cooperation among all the peoples of the Holy Land." Soon after his homily, however, the service was interrupted for a number of minutes as the Muslim call for prayer blared from the muezzin of the Mosque of Omar. His Holiness waited in silence before resuming the Mass. Later his spokesman noted that the local Muslim community had abbreviated its routine call for prayer in what he called an "unusual example of interreligious dialogue."

After the Mass, regional Christian scout groups serenaded the pope with their enthusiastic pipe-and-drum corps. This was surely an unusual sight for Westerners who may not have realized that the local Christian community was Arab and also that they would be dressed up

like Western Scouts playing Western instruments—bag-
pipes even! However, these customs, recent as they are,
derive from the British Mandate period (1920–47) when
British customs influenced much of the local population.

Finally the pope entered the Church of the Nativity
itself to descend into the cave that marks the traditional site
of Jesus' birth. There, in the crypt of this ancient church,
after greeting the local Greek Orthodox monks who have so
faithfully maintained the site through these many centuries, he prayed privately, both from his breviary and in
silent prayer.

As much as he insisted on the spiritual nature of his
visit, the pope did not wish to appear simply as if he had
"parachuted" into the holy sites without acknowledging
something of the local situation. This he would do by showing his pastoral care for the local community in the refugee
camp known as Dheisheh, which was just south of
Bethlehem. There in a much less organized way, the Holy
Father met with those whose poverty is all too evident. The
camp, one of three in the Bethlehem area, is home for over
ten thousand, all Muslim and 40 percent under the age of
eighteen. Many have remarked that this pope has been concerned for the suffering of the Palestinian people right from
the beginning of his pontificate. When speaking with them
at Dheisheh, he said,

> You have been deprived of many things which repre-
> sent basic needs of the human person: proper housing,
> health care, education and work. Above all you bear
> the sad memory of what you were forced to leave
> behind, not just material possessions, but your free-

dom, the closeness of relatives, and the familiar surroundings and cultural tradition which nourished
your personal and family life.

He reiterated his own support for a Palestinian homeland and he pleaded "with all who are sincerely working
for justice and peace not to lose heart." Sad to report,
however, his words were not translated into Arabic for the
sake of the camp dwellers.

Many had hoped that the pope would be more forth-
coming, more partisan in his upholding of the Palestinian
aspirations for justice and peace. However, here, as in so
many other places, Pope John Paul had supported the
good and the right without casting blame. As British journalist Trevor Mostyn assessed,

> both Palestinians and Israelis tried to manipulate the
> Dheisheh visit, and a streamer placed above the pope and
> Arafat proclaimed that "Palestinians have the right of
> return." Some Palestinians maintained that the pope was
> saying nothing new if he did not utter these magic words.
> Not to be bullied by either side, he did not do so, any more
> that at Yad Vashem he was willing to blame the Catholic
> Church as an institution for the Holocaust, a confession
> that Israelis sought but one he could not give.[21]

Before leaving Bethlehem, as a final gift to His
Holiness, Chairman Arafat, who many times had met
with the pope in the Vatican, offered him a special gift: an

---

21. Trevor Mostyn, "Are These the Seeds of a Miracle?" *The Tablet*, April
1, 2000 .

antique depiction of the stations of the cross, made of mother of pearl, a local craft. When the chairman mentioned that there are fourteen stations of the cross, His Holiness replied, "There is a fifteenth—the Resurrection."

DAY FOUR: Jerusalem and Yad Vashem

Because of its small size and because of the pope's intense eucharistic devotion, the Cenacle on Jerusalem's Mount Zion would welcome only His Holiness and a few bishops and aides for a private Mass. The Cenacle, or Upper Room, is the traditional site for the Last Supper and the descent of the Holy Spirit upon the apostles, the latter known also as the Pentecost event. Pope John Paul chose the Cenacle as the place where he would sign his annual letter of encouragement to the world's Catholic priests, traditionally issued on Holy Thursday.[22]

Between the two singularly emotional moments on Mount Zion and at Yad Vashem, Pope John Paul II met with the two chief rabbis of Israel, and then made a courtesy visit to the president of Israel at his residence in West Jerusalem. Along with various government officials, President Ezer Weizman graciously said, "There is a question whether history makes a leader, or a leader creates history. You, Your Holiness, without doubt, clearly leave your mark and influence on history....You, Your Holiness, through your character, your conduct, and your personal influence, unite the hearts of humanity."

22. Pope John Paul II, "Rediscovering the Priesthood in Light of the Eucharist," *Origins* 29 (13 April 2000): 43:693ff.

In reply, His Holiness affirmed his commitment to a new relationship between the Catholic Church and the Jewish people:

History, as the ancients held, is the *Magistra vitae*, a teacher of how to live. This is why we must be determined to heal the wounds of the past, so that they may never be open again. We must work for a new era of reconciliation and peace between Jews and Christians. My visit is a pledge that the Catholic Church will do everything possible to ensure that this is not just a dream but a reality.

Most observers and commentators cite his visit to Yad Vashem, the memorial and museum of the *Shoah* in West Jerusalem, as the most highly charged of many moving moments in the papal journey to the Holy Land. In the solemn Hall of Remembrance, Pope John Paul greeted several *Shoah* survivors. Contrary to usual papal protocol whereby the pope sits in a grand chair and receives visitors, the Holy Father went one by one to the survivors. Here the image of the pope—frail, hobbling, himself a survivor of the *Shoah*—going to each survivor at Yad Vashem stunned and moved all who were all watching. When the Holy Father met survivor Edith Tzirer who squeezed and held his hand for more than a few moments, tears streaming down her cheek, the country experienced a corporate gasp of emotion.[23] This electric

---

23. A press release issued by Yad Vashem at the time of the papal visit described the woman as follows: "On the day of liberation, Edith [Tzirer] was lying next to the camp fence, suffering from tuberculosis and totally drained

moment eclipsed his speech, which was to follow.
Speculation had run rife through the Israeli press for days
beforehand: Would the pope "go beyond" the March 12th
expression of regret for historical offenses against the
Jews through the ages? Would he "apologize" for the
Holocaust? Again Israeli journalist Yossi Klein Halevi got
it right when he wrote:

> The pope's decisive breakthrough with Israelis
> occurred during his visit to Yad Vashem...As the pope
> moved among the elderly Holocaust survivors from
> Wadowice, Israelis forgot the apology issue; suddenly
> "Christian love" didn't seem an oxymoron. The next
> morning's headlines in the Hebrew press all focused on
> the pope's solidarity with Jewish suffering; none
> emphasized the absence of yet another apology.[24]

True, Pope John Paul II had not gone "beyond" what
the Church said in its 1998 document "We Remember" or
the previous week's seeking of forgiveness at St. Peter's
Basilica in Rome. The pope said he had simply

> come to Yad Vashem to pay homage to the millions of
> Jewish people who, stripped of everything, especially of
> their human dignity, were murdered in the Holocaust....

---

of strength. A young priest, Karol Wojtyla, gave her her first piece of bread
and a cup of hot tea. He carried her on his back for 3 km, from the camp to
the railway station where she joined other survivors. After staying in an
orphanage in Cracow, Edith was sent to a sanatorium in France to recuper-
ate. In 1951 she emigrated to Israel, where she married and raised a family.
Karol Wojtyla later became Pope John Paul II."

24. Yossi Klein Halevi, "Zionism's Gift," *The New Republic*, April 10,
2000, p. 6.

We wish to remember, but we wish to remember *for a purpose*, namely to ensure that never again will evil prevail, as it did for the millions of innocent victims of Nazism.

The rest of the day would be difficult for the Holy Father, but for quite different reasons. For weeks, local organizers had worked doggedly to bring together, in this city where "the air is thick with holiness," representatives of the three monotheistic religions. It looked as if it was going to happen at the Vatican's Notre Dame Center just outside of the Old City. The chief Ashkenazi rabbi, Rabbi Meir Lau, and the Muslim mufti would join the pope in an exchange of greetings and thoughts. Children's choirs would provide an attempt at interreligious harmony. But on the day before the event, the mufti pulled out of the commitment and sent in his place a judge from the local Islamic court. After Rabbi Lau claimed that the pope's presence indicated his endorsement of Israel's claim over Jerusalem—loudly hooted at by the Palestinian members of the audience—the Muslim judge went into a tirade about Israeli occupation and persecution of the Palestinians. Soon after he took his seat, the judge leaned over to the Holy Father to say that he had to leave for another engagement. Both these unfortunate attempts to score political points with their respective constituencies were met with the pope's calling for interreligious dialogue and understanding. "Religion is not, and must not become, an excuse for violence, particularly when religious identity coincides with cultural and ethnic identity. *Religion and peace go together!* Religious belief and practice cannot be separated from the defense of *the image of God in every human being."*

As many observed, there is still a long road ahead for such understanding.

DAY FIVE: The Galilee, Place of Jesus' Ministry

Day Five would see the pope's one outdoor Mass during his pilgrimage. Significantly he had chosen the Mount of Beatitudes on the northern shore of the Sea of Galilee where Jesus, according to the Gospel of Matthew, had taught the crowds the core part of his teaching. While all were welcome, during the Mass and sermon the Holy Father spoke, as on so many of his other trips, specifically to today's youth. Thousands had been bused up from the south—the West Bank near Jerusalem—and still more thousands from the most Christian part of Israel, the Galilee region itself. In addition, thousands of pilgrims had come from parts of Europe, many organized by the Neocatechumenal Way, which had responsibility for the Mount of Beatitudes celebration. The crowd's devotion and stamina were tested by the wind, cold, and rain of the morning. Finally, after an hour's delay, some sun shone through and the Mass began.

In his homily, not far from the place where Jesus had first put forward the Beatitudes, the Holy Father strongly challenged the young people of the twenty-first century to resist those voices that call for violence, pride, and persecution and to follow rather the ennobling, but difficult way of Christ:

To put your faith in Jesus means choosing to believe what he says, no matter how strange it may seem, and choosing to reject the claims of evil, no matter how sensible or attractive they may seem....Young people of the Holy Land, young people of the world: answer the Lord with a heart that is willing and open! Willing and open like the heart of the greatest daughter of Galilee, Mary, the Mother of Jesus.

The pope's day was filled out with private visits to the Church of the Multiplication of the Loaves at Tabgha, the adjacent Church of the Primacy of Peter, and the Shrine of the House of St. Peter in Capernaum. Pope John Paul returned by helicopter to the apostolic nuncio's house on the Mount of Olives in East Jerusalem for his well-deserved evening's rest.

DAY SIX: Nazareth, Place of Jesus' Youth

While Bethlehem is the place of Jesus' birth, Nazareth might be considered the place of the incarnation itself, the place where, through the message of an angel and the overshadowing of the Holy Spirit, the Word became flesh. The pope first prayed privately where Western Christians believe the angel Gabriel spoke to the Virgin Mary (Eastern Christians follow a tradition placing the announcement at the village spring a few hundred yards to the east). Then Pope John Paul II celebrated the Mass of the Annunciation with thousands of local Christians in the Franciscan Church of the Annunciation. In the atmosphere of this great mystery, the Holy Father urged the faithful to pray to Mary for "a great renewal of faith in all the children of the Church. A deep renewal of faith: not just as a general attitude of life, but as a conscious and courageous profession of the Creed." The atmosphere of Jesus' hometown also conjures up many images of the Holy Family's life. So the pope also prayed that "the Holy Family...inspire all Christians to *defend the family against so many present-day threats to its nature, its stability and its mission.*"

Following a meeting with the consuls general of the apostolic delegation in Jerusalem, Pope John Paul, now back in Jerusalem, made a private visit to the Church of All Nations in the Kidron Valley, the traditional site of Jesus' agony in the Garden of Gethsemane on the night before he died. As in the cave of Bethlehem, the pope sought a few moments to pray as a solitary pilgrim, but the quiet was underscored by the clatter of a thousand camera shutters. Then a ladder crashed to the floor and a woman, in a moment of religious ecstasy, started to read from scripture through a bullhorn. The pope hardly stirred at all. What had been observed so many times through the pilgrimage and, indeed, throughout his pontificate, was John Paul's ability—one must say *gift*—of being able to enter into a lonely, private place with the Lord, oblivious to the crash of the world around him. If any evidence was needed as to the "real purpose" of his pilgrimage to the Holy Land, these moments of private prayer, like those at the Cenacle and later Golgotha, should have made it quite clear. This pilgrim came to the Holy Land first to pray.

Finally on that day, Pope John Paul, again taking the initiative as he had at Yad Vashem, went this time to the Greek Orthodox Patriarch's residence in the Old City of Jerusalem. Ecumenical relations emanating from the local patriarch have not always been cordial. Centuries of rivalries with Rome, coupled with long memories of attempted convert-making by Western Christians, make local Orthodox wary of ecumenical outreach. Indeed, the month before, at the Greek Orthodox monastery at Mount Sinai, the monks declined to pray with the pontiff during his pilgrimage there. Undaunted and committed to new relations of good will with the Greek Orthodox, Pope John Paul happily accepted the local patriarch's invitation to meet him at his headquarters in the Old City. Apparently the drama of the moment and the genuine sincerity of John Paul moved the very feeble Patriarch Diodoros, who reflected genuine, surprising warmth and acceptance. Indeed, he strayed from his prepared text when he on the spur-of-the moment thanked the pope for his visit "from the bottom of our hearts." John Paul, recalling the historic Holy Land encounter between his predecessor Paul VI and Athenagoras, also went beyond his script as he invited all present to say the Lord's Prayer each in his own language. Thus they were able to pray together without actually saying the same words at the same time. (One has to understand that progress in this part of the world is measured in small increments.)

Many Greeks feel that their distinctive and traditional expression of Christianity is threatened by the large communities from the West. And so in many places they have resisted new cooperation with other churches. Pope John Paul sought to reassure them when he said,

> the ecclesial note of universality fully respects legitimate diversity. The variety and beauty of your liturgical rites, and of your spiritual, theological and canonical traditions and institutions, testifies to the richness of the divinely revealed and undivided heritage of the universal Church, as it has developed down the centuries in the East and in the West. There exists a legitimate diversity which in no way is opposed to the unity of the Body of Christ, but rather enhances the splendour of the Church and contributes greatly to the fulfillment of her mission. None of this wealth must be lost in the fuller unity to which we aspire.

DAY SEVEN: A Last Day in Jerusalem

The official day of pilgrimage and meeting began with a short encounter with the Great Mufti Sheikh Akram Sabri on the Temple Mount. There Pope John Paul thanked the common "God revered by Jews, Christians and Muslims. Jerusalem is the Holy City par excellence. It forms part of the common patrimony of our religions and of the whole of humanity."

This rather spare and simple moment was followed by perhaps the most unforgettable moment of the entire pilgrimage, a visit by Pope John Paul II to the Western— sometimes called "Wailing"—Wall. There, speaking on behalf of the Israeli government, Rabbi Michael Melchior noted the wall's character so very sacred to the Jewish people and their return to *eretz Israel.*

> We welcome your coming here as the realization of a commitment of the Catholic Church to end the era of hatred, humiliation, and persecution of the Jewish people....No longer may we pervert the sublime values of religion, to justify war. No longer may we call God's name, as we strike down those created in His image.

After accepting from Rabbi Melchior a specially inscribed Bible, Pope John Paul shuffled away from the clique of dignitaries to the Wall itself where in its cracks he placed a request for forgiveness for all the ways Christians through the ages have hurt the Jewish people. In his note, he used the same text proclaimed two weeks before in the Mass of forgiveness at St. Peter's Basilica in Rome (see page 10). In this simple, untrumpeted gesture—the first time a pope has prayed at the Western Wall—provided, I think, the most profound and lasting catechesis of the Israeli people about contemporary Catholic teaching about Jews and Judaism that has occurred in fifty years.[25] There at the Wall he prayed, not as a Jew, but as a Christian at the Jews' most sacred site. Rabbi Melchior later reflected, "As I accompanied the pope to the podium my perception was that the Pontiff was as if magnetized by the power of the Western Wall. When he touched the Wall I sensed that the Wall was

---

25. The short prayer is now on display at Yad Vashem.

indeed moving in the Pontiff's direction and was coming to touch Him."[26]

If the Western Wall is the holiest place on earth for Jews and the Temple Mount the third-holiest place on earth for Muslims (after Mecca and Medina), then the Church of the Holy Sepulcher (more aptly referred to as the Church of the Resurrection by the Orthodox) is the holiest place on earth for Christians. Pope John Paul would visit there twice on his last day in Jerusalem.

A characteristic of the Church of the Holy Sepulcher that surprises many from the West—besides its ancient, cluttered, unfocused ambience—is that it houses not only the traditional site of Jesus' resurrection, but also that of his crucifixion. Many Christians know that a crucifixion could not occur within the city, and so they wonder how Golgotha, like the tomb, can be located within the Old City walls. The answer is simple, if not obvious: the considerable walls in Jerusalem today mostly date from the mid-sixteenth century, commissioned and overseen by Sulieman the Magnificent. At the time of Jesus, this site was indeed outside the walls. So Pope John Paul chose it as the culmination of his pilgrimage to the Holy Land and as a site for one final Mass.

After praying at the Stone of Anointing, whereon tradition claims that Jesus' body was anointed prior to his burial, Pope John Paul proceeded to the Holy Sepulcher itself where the Mass took place. He reflected:

---

26. As translated and quoted from his article in *L'Osservatore Romano*, March 22, 2000, in *SIDIC* 34, no. 1, p. 7.

Here, where our Lord Jesus Christ died in order to gather into one the children of God who were scattered, may the Father of mercies strengthen our desire for unity and peace among all who have received the gift of new life through the saving waters of Baptism....The good news of the Resurrection can never be separated from the mystery of the Cross....The Resurrection of Jesus is the definitive seal of all God's promises, the birthplace of a new, risen humanity.

But even as the pope left the massive church on his way to the Latin (Roman Catholic) Patriarchate for lunch and a further meeting with leaders of other Churches (most notably the local Armenian Patriarch, His Beatitude Torkom Manoogian), one had the feeling that John Paul had not drunk deeply enough of the central Christian mystery encased in the church. During the time allotted for a rest after lunch, the pope told his aides that he wished to return to the church for prayer, for time alone in the Chapel of Calvary. After security personnel hastily assembled, Pope John Paul returned to the Church of the Holy Sepulcher and struggled up the twenty-two very steep steps to Calvary for time alone. Once again, the pilgrim had sought solitary time for prayer.

Concluding Thoughts

Was the trip of the Holy Father a success? Well, as in many life issues, it depends on whom you talk to. True, some Israelis and some Palestinians had tried, sometimes subtly, sometimes not, to politicize the journey. Whether it was the words of a rabbi ascribing Pope John Paul's presence as an affirmation of a particular Israeli political position or a Muslim cleric using an interreligious meeting as a platform for a political harangue, somehow Pope John Paul avoided the proverbial explosions in the minefield. But his words still spoke strongly, whether in condemning anti-semitism or seeking justice for the Palestinian people or rights for the beleaguered Christian minority. How was he able to do this? Juan Navarro-Valls, the papal spokesman, explained: "The key thing, I think, was that the pope told the truth to everyone, but without humiliating anyone. He spoke in charity...and people respected that."[27]

Before the pilgrimage, I myself had felt rather realistic, even low, prospects for the papal journey to the Holy Land. My experience of papal visits to cities in the United States may have jaded me. But, like the Palestinian and Israeli expectations reflected in the English-language press, I began to change as his arrival got close. Hard-core Jewish and Muslim religious sentiments seemed ready not to be influenced in any way. And one might ask, Why should they have been? The centrality of the pope as a religious leader is certainly well known, even overplayed in the West. Here in the Middle East, other and more complex dynamics hold sway, so one would have had to be unaware of these factors to think that a papal visit would substantially change realities on the ground—and these for reasons I have already spoken about above. Nonetheless, I must say that certain moments in the papal visit were overwhelm-

---

27. John Thavis, "Reflections on the Journey," *Catholic Life* (May/June 2000):44:35.

ingly moving, not only to me but also to those around me. Many, but not all, Palestinian Christians I know felt that Pope John Paul had lifted up their concerns for the world to see. Israeli Jews open to dialogue and new expressions of understanding were incredibly moved by the three iconic moments I have already enumerated: the handshake with Prime Minister Barak at the airport, the meeting with *Shoah* survivors at Yad Vashem, and the Holy Father's placing in the Western Wall the expression of Catholic regret for all transgressions of the Christian people against Jews. As one rabbi eloquently put it, "He touched the wall and the wall touched him." As with his visit to the Rome synagogue in 1986, what was remembered by those who live here in the Holy Land—whether in Palestine, Jordan, or Israel— were not so much the pope's words as his actions.

It was my work to provide "color commentary" for the American networks of MSNBC, NBC, and CNBC during the papal visit and that was a great privilege—to frame the meaning of the pope's visits to various places in the Holy Land. At the same time, I was amazed by the reaction of highly professional but furiously busy media people. In the cramped, cluttered rooms that passed for television studios in the Jerusalem Hilton, people conscientiously went about their work. But when the pope approached the Holocaust survivors, or when he shuffled toward the Wall, or as his helicopter circled over the Old City of Jerusalem on its way to Ben Gurion airport, a hush descended on the otherwise-bustling engineers. They listened intently to this old man, this pilgrim, as they keenly yearned for signs of hope in their own world often surfeited by the superficial, the slick, and the spin. I was dumbfounded. Maybe this was the effect of the trip: for people from all walks of life and religious traditions to be moved by a man obviously overwhelmed by his own faith, beyond the suasions of trends and fads, seeking understanding, peace, and justice.

But the final evaluation must be left to the one who planned the trip and who reflected on it afterward in his Apostolic Letter *Novo Millennio Ineunte*:

> It is difficult to express the emotion I felt in being able to venerate the places of [Jesus'] birth and life, Bethlehem and Nazareth, to celebrate the Eucharist in the Upper Room, in the very place of its institution, to meditate again on the mystery of the cross at Golgotha where he gave his life for us. In those places, still so troubled and again recently afflicted by violence, I received an extraordinary welcome not only from the members of the church but also from the Israeli and Palestinian communities. Intense emotion surrounded my prayer at the Western Wall and my visit to the mausoleum of Yad Vashem, with its chilling reminder of the victims of the Nazi death camps. My pilgrimage was a moment of brotherhood and peace, and I like to remember it as one of the most beautiful gifts of the whole jubilee event. Thinking back to the mood of those days, I cannot but express my deeply felt desire for a prompt and just solution to the still unresolved problems of the holy places, cherished by Jews, Christians and Muslims together.[28]

---

28. Pope John Paul II, "Apostolic Letter '*Novo Millenio Ineunte*,'" *Origins* 30 (January 18, 2001): 31:489–508, at 494–495.

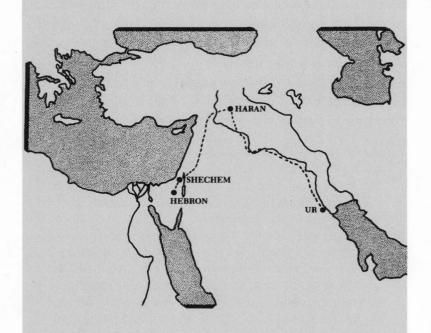

The pope's *spiritual pilgrimage* to Ur from Rome
February 23, 2000

The pilgrimage really begins with these places
the pope could not visit due to violence.

John Paul II at the Church of the Primacy of Peter, also known as the *Mensa Christi*, where Jesus' postresurrection appearance recounted in John 21:3–15 is commemorated.

Flanked by Church officials, Pope John Paul II prays at the traditional Latin Catholic site for the Annunciation. Here, Mary was visited by the angel Gabriel, who told her that she would be the mother of the Messiah (Luke 1:26–38).

Pope John Paul II approaches the Western Wall, accompanied by then Minister of Diaspora Affairs, Rabbi Michael Melchior.

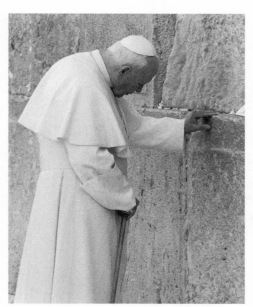

Pope John Paul II alone at the Western Wall saying the prayer seeking forgiveness.

The prayer for forgiveness is placed in the Western Wall by the Supreme Pontiff.

A picture of the prayer left by Pope John Paul II in the Western Wall.

Pope John Paul II meets Chief Ashkenazi Rabbi Israel Meir Lau (also a native of Poland and a *Shoah* survivor, left) and Chief Sephardic Rabbi Eliahu Bakshi-Doron (right).

His Holiness flanked by Chief Ashkenazi Rabbi Israel Meir Lau and Muslim cleric Taysir al-Tamini at the Notre Dame of Jerusalem Center for Interreligious Events.

Pope John Paul II presides at the outdoor Mass near the Mount of Beatitudes (March 24).

The Holy Land in the time of Jesus

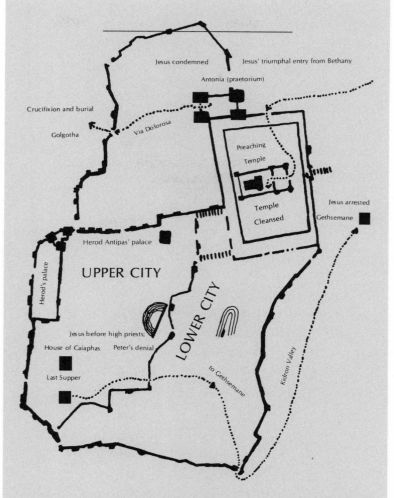

A map of the Holy City, Jerusalem, indicating
where Jesus was before, during, and after his crucifixion.

Pope John Paul ll's Homilies and Messages from the Holy Land

1. Commemoration of Abraham, "Our Father in Faith," in Paul VI Hall, the Vatican

February 23, 2000

1. "I am the Lord who brought you from Ur of the Chaldeans, to give you this land to possess....On that day the Lord made a covenant with Abraham, saying: 'To your descendants I give this land, from the river of Egypt to the great river, the river Euphrates'" (Gen 15:7, 18).

Before Moses heard Yahweh's well-known words on Mount Sinai: "I am the Lord your God, who brought you out of the land of Egypt, out of the house of bondage" (Exod 20:2), the patriarch Abraham had already heard these other words: "I am the Lord who brought you from Ur of the Chaldeans." Therefore, our thoughts must turn to that important place in the history of God's People, to seek there the origins of God's covenant with [us]. This is why, during this year of the Great Jubilee, as our hearts return to the beginnings of God's covenant with humanity, *we turn our gaze to Abraham,* to the place where he heard God's call and responded to it with the obedience of faith. Together with us, Jews and Muslims also look to the person of Abraham as a model of unconditional submission to the will of God (*Nostra Aetate,* n. 3).

The author of the Letter to the Hebrews writes: "By faith Abraham obeyed when he was called to go out to a place which he was to receive as an inheritance; and he went out, not knowing where he was to go" (Heb 11:8). Behold: Abraham, whom the Apostle calls "our father in faith" (Rom 4:11–16), believed in God, trusted in the One who called him. *He believed in his promise.* God said to Abraham: "Go from your country and your kindred and your father's house to the land that I will show you. And I will make of you a great nation, and I will bless you, and make your name great, so that you will be a blessing....By you all the families of the earth shall bless themselves" (Gen 12:1–3). Are we talking about the route taken by one of the many migrations typical of an era when sheep-rearing was a basic form of economic life? Probably. Surely though, *it was not only this.* In Abraham's life, which marks the beginning of salvation history, we can already perceive another meaning of the call and the promise. The land to which human beings, guided by the voice of God, are moving, *does not belong exclusively to the geography of this world.* Abraham, the believer who accepts God's invitation, is someone heading toward a promised land that is not of this world.

2. In the Letter to the Hebrews we read: "By faith Abraham, when he was tested, offered up Isaac, and he who had received the promises was ready to offer up his only son, of whom it was said, "Through Isaac shall your

descendants be named'" (11:17–18). *This is the climax of Abraham's faith.* Abraham is tested by that God in whom he had placed his trust, that God from whom he had received the promise about the distant future: "Through Isaac shall your descendants be named" (Heb 11:18). He is called, however, to offer in sacrifice to God precisely that Isaac, his only son, on whom his every hope is based, in accordance moreover with the divine promise. How could God's promise to him of numerous descendants come true if Isaac, his only son, were to be offered in sacrifice?

Through faith Abraham emerges victorious from this test, a dramatic test that challenged his faith directly. "He considered," writes the author of the Letter to the Hebrews, "that God was able to raise men even from the dead" (11:9). At that humanly tragic moment, when he was ready to inflict the mortal blow on his son, Abraham never stopped believing. Indeed, his faith in God's promise reached its climax. He thought that "God was able to raise men even from the dead." This is what this father, tested humanly speaking beyond all measure, thought. And his faith, his total abandonment to God, did not disappoint him. It is written: "hence he did receive him back" (Heb 1:19). Isaac was given back to him because he believed in God completely and unconditionally.

The author of the Letter seems to express something more here: all of Abraham's experience appears to him as *an analogy of the saving event of Christ's death and resurrection.* This man, placed at the origins of our faith, is part of God's eternal plan. There is a tradition that the place where Abraham was to have sacrificed his own son is the very same place where another father, the eternal Father, would accept the offering of his Only-begotten Son, Jesus Christ. Thus Abraham's sacrifice can be seen as a prophetic sign of Christ's sacrifice. St John writes: "For God so loved the world that he gave his only Son" (John 3:16). The patriarch Abraham, our father in faith, unknowingly brings all believers, in a certain sense, into God's eternal plan in which the world's redemption is accomplished.

3. One day Christ said: "Truly, truly, I say to you, before Abraham was, I am" (John 8:58), and these words astonished his listeners, who objected: "You are not yet fifty years old, and have you seen Abraham?" (John 8:57). Those who reacted so reasoned in a merely human way, and therefore did not accept what Christ said. "Are you greater than our father Abraham, who died? And the prophets died! Who do you claim to be?" (John 8:53). Jesus answered them: "Your father Abraham rejoiced that he was to see my day; he saw it and was glad" (John 8:56). Abraham's vocation seems entirely directed to the day of which Christ is speaking. Here human calculations fail; *God's measure must be applied.* Only then can we understand the proper meaning of the obedience of Abraham who "believed against hope" (Rom 4:18). He hoped to become the father of many nations, and today he is certainly rejoicing with us because God's promise is fulfilled down the centuries, from generation to generation.

His believing, hoping against hope, was "reckoned to him as righteousness" (Rom 4:22), not only in his regard, but in view of us all, his descendants in faith. We "believe in him that raised from the dead Jesus our Lord" (Rom 4:24), put to death for our sins and raised for our justification (Rom 4:25). Abraham did not know this, but through the obedience of faith he directed his steps toward the fulfillment of all the divine promises, motivated by the hope that they would come to pass. Is there any greater promise than that fulfilled in Christ's paschal mystery? In the faith of Abraham almighty God truly made an eternal covenant with the human race, and its definitive fulfillment is Jesus Christ. The Only-begotten Son of the Father, one in substance with him, became Man to lead us through the humiliation of the cross and the glory of the resurrection into the land of salvation that God, rich in mercy, had promised humanity from the very beginning.

4. Mary, "who believed that there would be a fulfillment of what was spoken to her from the Lord" (Luke 1:45), is an unsurpassable model of the redeemed people on their way to the fulfillment of this universal promise.

Daughter of Abraham in faith as well as in the flesh, Mary personally shared in this experience. Like Abraham, she too accepted the sacrifice of her Son, but while the actual sacrifice of Isaac was not demanded of Abraham, Christ drank the cup of suffering to the last drop. Mary personally took part in her Son's trial, believing and hoping at the foot of the cross (John 19:25).

This was the epilogue of a long wait. Having been taught to meditate on the prophetic texts, Mary foresaw what awaited her and in praising the mercy of God, faithful to his people from generation to generation, she gave her own consent to his plan of salvation; in particular, she said her "yes" to the central event of this plan, the sacrifice of that Child whom she bore in her womb. Like Abraham, she accepted the sacrifice of her Son.

Today we join our voice to hers and with her, Virgin Daughter of Zion, we proclaim that God has remembered his mercy, "as he spoke to our fathers, to Abraham and to his posterity for ever" (Luke 1:55).

2. Address upon Arrival in Egypt

February 24, 2000

Mr. President,
Your Holiness Pope Shenouda,
Your Beatitude Patriarch Stephanos,
Grand Sheikh Mohammed Sayed Tantawi,
Dear People of Egypt,

As-salám 'aláikum—Peace be with you!

1. For many years I have been looking forward to celebrating the 2000th anniversary of the birth of Jesus Christ by visiting and praying at the places specially linked to God's interventions in history. My Jubilee pilgrimage brings me today to Egypt. Thank you, Mr. President, for making it possible for me to come here and to go to where God revealed his name to Moses and gave his Law as a sign of his great mercy and kindness toward his creatures. I greatly appreciate your kind words of welcome.

This is the land of a five thousand-year-old civilization known throughout the world for its monuments and for its knowledge of mathematics and astronomy. This is the land where different cultures met and mingled, making Egypt famous for its wisdom and learning.

2. In Christian times, the city of Alexandria—where the Church was established by the disciple of Peter and Paul, the evangelist Mark—nurtured renowned ecclesiastical writers like Clement and Origen, and great Fathers of the Church such as Athanasius and Cyril. The fame of Saint Catherine of Alexandria lives on in Christian devotion and in the name of many churches in all parts of the world. Egypt, with Saints Anthony and Pachomius, was the birthplace of monasticism, which has played an essential part in preserving the spiritual and cultural traditions of the Church.

The advent of Islam brought splendors of art and learning, which have had a determining influence on the Arab world and on Africa. The people of Egypt have for centuries pursued the ideal of national unity. Differences of religion were never barriers, but a form of mutual enrichment in the service of the one national community. I well remember the words of Pope Shenouda III: "Egypt is not the native land in which we live, but the native land which lives in us."

3. The unity and harmony of the nation are a precious value that all citizens should cherish, and that political and religious leaders must continually promote in justice and respect for the rights of all. Mr. President, your own commitment to peace at home and throughout the Middle East is well known. You have been instrumental in advancing the peace process in the region. All reasonable

men and women appreciate the efforts made so far, and hope that goodwill and justice will prevail, so that all the peoples of this unique area of the world will see their rights respected and their legitimate aspirations fulfilled.

My visit to Saint Catherine's Monastery at the foot of Mount Sinai will be a moment of intense prayer for peace and for interreligious harmony. To do harm, to promote violence and conflict in the name of religion, is a terrible contradiction and a great offence against God. But past and present history gives us many examples of such a misuse of religion. We must all work to strengthen the growing commitment to interreligious dialogue, a great sign of hope for the peoples of the world.

As-salám 'aláikum—Peace be with you!

This is my greeting to you all. This is the prayer I offer up for Egypt and all her people.

May the Most High God bless your land with harmony, peace and prosperity.

3. Homily at Mass in Cairo Sport Palace

February 25, 2000

1. "Out of Egypt have I called my son" (Matt 2:15).

Today's Gospel recalls the flight of the Holy Family into Egypt where they came to seek refuge. "An angel of the Lord appeared to Joseph in a dream and said, 'Rise, take the child and his mother, and flee to Egypt, and remain there till I tell you: for Herod is about to search for the child, to destroy him'" (Matt 2:13). In this way, Christ too, "who became [hu]man so that [humanity] could receive the divinity" (Saint Athanasius of Alexandria, *Contra Arianos*, 2, 59), wished to retrace the journey which was that of the divine call, the route which his people had taken so that all the members of the people could become sons and daughters in the Son. Joseph "rose and took the child and his mother by night, and departed to Egypt, and remained there until the death of Herod. This was to fulfill what the Lord had spoken by the prophet, 'Out of Egypt have I called my son'" (Matt 2:14–15). Providence led Jesus along the paths upon which in former times the Israelites had marched to go toward the Promised Land, under the sign of the paschal lamb, celebrating the Passover. Jesus, the Lamb of God, too was called out of Egypt by the Father to fulfill in Jerusalem the Passover of the new and irrevocable covenant, the definitive Passover, which gives salvation to the world.

2. "Out of Egypt have I called my son." Thus speaks the Lord, who brought his people out of the condition of slavery (Exod 20:2) to establish a covenant with them at Mount Sinai. The Passover feast would always be the remembrance of that liberation. It commemorates this event, which remains present in the memory of the people of God. When the Israelites departed for their long march, under the leadership of Moses, they did not think that their wanderings in the desert would last for forty years until they reached the Promised Land. Moses himself, who had led his people out of Egypt and had guided it throughout this time, did not enter the Promised Land. Before he died, he only contemplated it from the height of

Mount Nebo, before handing on responsibility for the people to his successor Joshua.

3. While Christians are celebrating the two-thousandth anniversary of the birth of Jesus, we must make this pilgrimage to the places that saw the beginning and unfolding of the history of salvation, the history of the irrevocable love between God and men, the Lord's presence in time and in human lives. We have come to Egypt, on the path upon which God guided his people, with Moses as their leader, to bring them into the Promised Land. We are setting out, guided by the words of the book of Exodus. Leaving our condition of slavery, we are going toward Mount Sinai, where God sealed his covenant with the house of Jacob, through Moses, in whose hands he placed the tables of the Decalogue. How beautiful is this covenant! It shows that God does not stop speaking to [us] in order to give [us] life in abundance. It places us in the presence of God and is the expression of his profound love for his people. It invites [us] to turn to God, to allow [us] to be touched by God's love and to fulfill the desire for happiness which [we] bear within [ourselves]. If we accept wholeheartedly the tables of the Ten Commandments, we will live fully by the law which God has placed in our hearts and we will have a share in the salvation which the covenant made on Mount Sinai between God and his people revealed, and which the Son of God through his work of redemption offer to us.

4. In this land of Egypt, which I have the joy of visiting for the first time, the message of the new covenant has been transmitted from generation to generation through

the venerable Coptic Church, heir to the apostolic preaching and activity of the evangelist Saint Mark who, according to tradition, suffered martyrdom in Alexandria. On this day, let us give fervent thanks to God for the rich history of the Church and for the generous apostolate of its faithful, who down the centuries have been ardent witnesses to the Lord's love, sometimes even to the point of shedding their blood.

With affection I thank His Beatitude Stephanos II Ghattas, Catholic Coptic Patriarch of Alexandria, for his words of welcome; they bear witness to your community's living faith and fidelity to the Church. I cordially greet the patriarchs and bishops who are taking part in this liturgy, as well as the priests, religious, and all the faithful who have come to accompany me in this stage of my Jubilee pilgrimage. I also extend respectful greetings to the authorities and all those who have wished to be present for this celebration.

Your presence here around the Successor of Peter is a sign of the unity of the Church of which Christ is the head. May the fraternity among all the Lord's followers, so clearly manifested here, encourage you to continue your efforts to build communities united in love, acting as a leaven of concord and reconciliation! In this way, you will find strength and comfort, especially in moments of difficulty or doubt, to bear ever more ardent witness to Christ in the land of your ancestors. With the apostle Paul, I give thanks to God, the Father of our Lord Jesus Christ, and I pray for you without ceasing so that you will grow in faith, be steadfast in hope, and spread everywhere the love of Christ (Col 1:3–5).

5. In this Jubilee year, as we recall that Christ is "the Head of the Body, the Church" (Col 1:18), we must seek ever more ardently to make resolute progress on the path of the unity that he willed for his disciples, in a spirit of trust and fraternity. In this way our common witness will give glory to God and be more credible in the eyes of men. I pray to our Heavenly Father that serene and fraternal relations, in charity and good will, will be developed with the Orthodox Coptic Church, which I greet here with respect. Such a climate of dialogue and reconciliation will help to find solutions to the problems that still impede full communion. It will also promote respect for the sensitivities of each community, as well as for their specific way of expressing their faith in Christ and celebrating the sacraments, which the Churches must reciprocally recognize as administered in the name of the same Lord. In celebrating the Passover of the Lord during this pilgrimage, may we relive the Pentecost experience, when all the disciples—gathered together with the Mother of God—received the Holy Spirit who reconciles us with the Lord and is the principle of unity and strength for mission, making of us one body, the image of the world to come!

6. From the beginning, spiritual and intellectual life developed in a remarkable way in the Church in Egypt. Here we may recall the illustrious founders of Christian monasticism: Anthony, Pachomius, and Macarius, and so many other patriarchs, confessors, thinkers, and doctors who are the glory of the universal Church. Even today the

monasteries are living centers of prayer, study, and meditation, in fidelity to the ancient cenobitic and anchoritic traditions of the Coptic Church, reminding us that faithful and prolonged contact with the Lord is the leaven that transforms individuals and society as a whole. Thus life with God causes the light to shine on our human faces and illumines the world with a new brightness, the living flame of love.

By accepting today this spiritual and apostolic enthusiasm handed down to them by their fathers in faith, may the young be attentive to the call of the Lord who invites them to follow him, and may they respond with generosity by committing themselves to him in the priesthood or the active or contemplative consecrated life! By the witness of their lives as men and women totally consecrated to God and their brothers and sisters, based on an intense spiritual experience, may consecrated men and women manifest the Lord's unlimited love for the world!

7. In her commitment to the Egyptian people in the areas of education, health, and charitable works, the Church seeks to express this disinterested love that excludes no one. The Church's active presence in the intellectual and moral formation of young people is a long tradition of the Coptic Patriarchate and the Latin Vicariate. Catholic educational institutions wish to contribute to the promotion of the human person, especially of women and the family, by educating young people in essential human, spiritual, and moral values, with respect for the conscience of everyone; they also aim at fostering friendly relations with Muslims so that the mem-

bers of each community may make sincere efforts to understand one another and promote together social justice, moral values, peace, respect, and freedom.

All citizens have a duty to play an active part, in a spirit of solidarity, in the building of society, in consolidating peace between communities, and in managing the common good in an honest way. In order to do this common work that should bring together all the members of the same nation, it is right that everyone, Christians and Muslims, while respecting different religious views, should place their skills at the service of the nation, at every level of society.

8. Following Moses in his journey of faith, during the Jubilee pilgrimage we are making in these days, we are invited to continue our way to the mountain of the Lord, to put aside our different forms of slavery in order to walk on the Lord's path. "And God, seeing our good decisions and observing that we ascribe to him what we achieve...will give us in return what is proper to him, the spiritual, divine, and heavenly gifts" (Saint Macarius, *Spiritual Homilies*, 26, 20). For each one of us, Horeb, the "mountain of faith," is to become "the place of encounter and of the mutual pact, in a sense therefore 'the mountain of love'" ("Letter Concerning Pilgrimage to the Places Linked to the History of Salvation," 6). This is where the people committed themselves to live in full accord with the divine will, and where God assured them of his eternal benevolence. This mystery of love is fulfilled in the Passover of the new covenant, in the gift which the Father makes of his Son for the salvation of all humanity.

Let us today renew our acceptance of the divine law as a precious treasure! Like Moses, let us become men and women who intercede before the Lord and pass on to others the law that is a call to true life, that frees us from idols and makes every life infinitely beautiful and infinitely precious! For their part, young people are impatiently waiting for us to help them to discover the face of God, to show them the path to follow, the path of personal encounter with God and the human acts worthy of our divine filiation, a path which is certainly demanding, but a path of liberation which alone will fulfill their desire for happiness. When we are with God on the mountain of prayer, may we allow ourselves to be penetrated by his light, so that our faces will shine with the glory of God and be an invitation to others to live by this divine beatitude, which is the fullness of life!

"Out of Egypt have I called my son." May everyone hear the call of the God of the covenant and discover the joy of being his sons and daughters!

4. Homily at St. Catherine's Monastery, Mount Sinai

February 26, 2000

Dear Brothers and Sisters,

1. In this year of the Great Jubilee, our faith leads us to become pilgrims in the footsteps of God. We contemplate the path he has taken through time, revealing to the world the magnificent mystery of his faithful Love for all

humankind. Today, with great joy and deep emotion, the Bishop of Rome is a pilgrim to Mount Sinai, drawn by this holy mountain that rises like a soaring monument to what God revealed here. Here he revealed his name! Here he gave his Law, the Ten Commandments of the covenant!

How many have come to this place before us! Here the People of God pitched their tents (Exod 19:2); here the prophet Elijah took refuge in a cave (1 Kgs 19:9); here the body of the martyr Catherine found a final resting-place; here a host of pilgrims through the ages have scaled what Saint Gregory of Nyssa called "the mountain of desire" (*The Life of Moses*, II, 232); here generations of monks have watched and prayed. We humbly follow in their footsteps to "the holy ground" where the God of Abraham, of Isaac, and of Jacob commissioned Moses to set his people free (Exod 3:5–8).

2. God shows himself in mysterious ways—as the fire that does not consume—according to a logic which defies all that we know and expect. He is the God who is at once close at hand and faraway; he is in the world but not of it. He is the God who comes to meet us, but who will not be possessed. He is "I AM WHO I AM"—the name that is no name! I AM WHO I AM: the divine abyss in which essence and existence are one! The God who is Being itself! Before such a mystery, how can we fail to "take off our shoes" as he commands, and adore him on this holy ground?

Here on Mount Sinai, the truth of "who God is" became the foundation and guarantee of the covenant. Moses enters "the luminous darkness" (*The Life of Moses*, II, 164), and there he is given the Law "written with the finger of God" (Exod 31:18). But what is this Law? It is the Law of life and freedom!

At the Red Sea, the people had experienced a great liberation. They had seen the power and fidelity of God; they had discovered that he is the God who does indeed set his people free as he had promised. But now on the heights of Sinai, this same God seals his love by making the covenant that he will never renounce. If the people obey his Law, they will know freedom forever. The exodus and the covenant are not just events of the past; they are forever the destiny of all God's people!

3. The encounter of God and Moses on this mountain enshrines at the heart of our religion the mystery of liberating obedience, which finds its fulfillment in the perfect obedience of Christ in the Incarnation and on the cross (see Phil 2:8; Heb 5:8–9). We too shall be truly free if we learn to obey as Jesus did (Heb 5:8).

The Ten Commandments are not an arbitrary imposition of a tyrannical Lord. They were written in stone; but before that, they were written on the human heart as the universal moral law, valid in every time and place. Today, as always, the Ten Words of the Law provide the only true basis for the lives of individuals, societies, and nations. Today, as always, they are the only future of the human family. They save man from the destructive force of egoism, hatred, and falsehood. They point out all the false gods that draw him into slavery: the love of self to the exclusion of God, the greed for power and pleasure that overturns the order of justice and degrades our human dignity and that of our neighbor. If we turn from these false idols and follow the God who sets his people free and remains always with them, then we shall emerge like Moses, after forty days on the mountain, "shining with glory" (Saint Gregory of Nyssa, *The Life of Moses*, II, 230), ablaze with the light of God!

To keep the Commandments is be faithful to God, but it is also to be faithful to ourselves, to our true nature and our deepest aspirations. The wind which still today blows from Sinai reminds us that God wants to be honored in and through the growth of his creatures: *Gloria Dei, homo vivens*. In this sense, that wind carries an insistent invitation to dialogue between the followers of the great monotheistic religions in their service of the human family. It suggests that in God we can find the point of our encounter: in God the All Powerful and All Merciful, Creator of the universe and Lord of history, who at the end of our earthly existence will judge us with perfect justice.

4. The Gospel reading that we have just listened to suggests that Sinai finds its fulfillment on another mountain, the Mountain of the Transfiguration, where Jesus appears to his apostles shining with the glory of God. Moses and Elijah stand with him to testify that the fullness of God's revelation is found in the glorified Christ.

On the Mountain of the Transfiguration, God speaks from the cloud, as he had done on Sinai. But now he says: "This is my beloved Son; listen to him" (Mark 9:7). He commands us to listen to his Son, because "no one knows the Father except the Son and anyone to whom the Son chooses to reveal him" (Matt 11:27). And so we learn that the true name of God is FATHER! The name which is beyond all other names: ABBA! (Gal 4:6). And in Jesus we learn that our true name is SON, DAUGHTER! We learn that the God of the exodus and the covenant sets his people free because they are his sons and daughters, created not for slavery but for "the glorious liberty of the children of God" (Rom 8:21).

So when Saint Paul writes that we "have died to the law through the body of Christ" (Rom 7:4), he does not mean that the Law of Sinai is past. He means that the Ten Commandments now make themselves heard through the voice of the Beloved Son. The person delivered by Jesus Christ into true freedom is aware of being bound not externally by a multitude of prescriptions, but internally by the love which has taken hold in the deepest recesses of his heart. The Ten Commandments are the law of freedom: not the freedom to follow our blind passions, but the freedom to love, to choose what is good in every situation, even when to do so is a burden. It is not an impersonal law that we obey; what is required is loving surrender to the Father through Christ Jesus in the Holy Spirit (see Rom 6:14; Gal 5:18). In revealing himself on the mountain and giving his Law, God revealed [us to ourselves]. Sinai stands at the very heart of the truth about [humanity] and [our] destiny.

5. In pursuit of this truth, the monks of this monastery pitched their tent in the shadow of Sinai. The Monastery of the Transfiguration and Saint Catherine bears all the marks of time and human turmoil, but it stands indomitable as a witness to divine wisdom and love. For centuries monks from all Christian traditions

lived and prayed together in this monastery, listening to the Word, in whom dwells the fullness of the Father's wisdom and love. In this very monastery, Saint John Climacus wrote *The Ladder of Divine Ascent*, a spiritual masterpiece that continues to inspire monks and nuns, from East and West, generation after generation. All this has taken place under the mighty protection of the Great Mother of God. As early as the third century, Egyptian Christians appealed to her with words of trust: We have recourse to your protection, O Holy Mother of God! *Sub tuum praesidium confugimus, sancta Dei Genetrix!* Through the centuries, this Monastery has been an exceptional meeting place for people belonging to different Churches, traditions, and cultures. I pray that in the new millennium the Monastery of Saint Catherine will be a radiant beacon calling the Churches to know one another better and to rediscover the importance in the eyes of God of the things that unite us in Christ.

6. I am grateful to the many faithful from the Diocese of Ismayliah, led by Bishop Makarios, who have come to join me in this pilgrimage to Mount Sinai. The Successor of Peter thanks you for your steadfastness in faith. God bless you and your families!

May the Monastery of Saint Catherine be a spiritual oasis for members of all the Churches in search of the glory of the Lord that settled on Mount Sinai (Exod 24:16). The vision of this glory prompts us to cry out in overflowing joy: "We give thanks to you, O holy Father, for your holy name, which you have made to dwell in our hearts" (*Didache*, X). Amen.

The Pope Follows the Pilgrim Rituals

While at Mount Sinai, the Holy Father also visited the Church of the Transfiguration at St. Catherine's Monastery. St. Catherine's is the oldest Christian monastery in the world, erected by the Roman emperor Justinian in 527. It is traditionally accepted as the site of the burning bush from which God spoke to Moses and revealed his name. Like Moses, the pope removed his shoes, knelt, and kissed the holy ground.

When honoring the relics of St. Catherine, the pope also followed in the steps of other pilgrims, and performed the ancient practice of putting his own ring on the finger of the saint's skeleton, touching the ring to the skull, and then putting it back on. John Paul also venerated the sixth-century *Christ Pantocrator,* one of the earliest surviving icons. Many believe this icon to have been copied from the Shroud of Turin, which at one time was in the Greek city of Odessa.

John Paul's visit to the monastery and its relics was a time of deep emotion and an intense spiritual experience.

5. Angelus Message, the Vatican

February 27, 2000

Dearest Brothers and Sisters!

1. I thank the Lord who, after the special commemoration of Abraham held in the Paul VI Auditorium last

Wednesday, enabled me to make these days of planned pilgrimage to Egypt, a hospitable land that gave refuge to the Holy Family fleeing from Herod, and that received the Gospel in apostolic times and is heir of a very ancient civilization. The high point of this pilgrimage was the ascent to Mount Sinai.

I am grateful to President Mubarak and to the Egyptian authorities, to the organizers, and to those who in different ways contributed to my making this visit in Moses' footsteps. I renew my thanks to the Coptic Orthodox Church, with whose patriarch, His Holiness Shenouda III, I had a cordial discussion; as well as Egumeno Damianos and the Greek-Orthodox monks, for their hospitality near Mount Sinai.

2. I send cordial greetings and appreciation to the fervent Catholic community, with whom on Friday I was able to celebrate a solemn Holy Mass in the Cairo Sports Palace, in which all the Churches present in Egypt took part: the Coptic, Latin, Maronite, Greek, Armenian, Syrian, and Chaldean.

A significant ecumenical meeting was later held in the new cathedral, consecrated last Christmas, with representatives and faithful of the Churches and ecclesial community present in Egypt. I am pleased to emphasize how profitable the dialogue with the Coptic Orthodox Church was, and I pray the Lord that he will render it ever richer in fruits of mutual understanding and collaboration.

I also want to thank Grand Sheikh Sayed Tantawi of Al-Azhar, head of the Muslim community to which the greater part of the population belongs, for our courteous meeting.

Now my thoughts turn to the central part of my pilgrimage, the most ancient Monastery of St. Catherine on Mount Sinai. There, in a simple but touching ceremony, I was able to commemorate both the moment in which God, speaking from the burning bush, revealed his name "I am" to Moses, and where he stipulated the covenant with the People, founded on the Decalogue. The fundamental precepts of the Natural Law are reflected in the Ten Commandments. The Decalogue points out the way for a fully human life. Outside of it there is no future of serenity and peace for persons, families, or nations.

3. My eyes now turn to the Holy Land, the land of Jesus Christ, where, God willing, I will go during the last week of the month of March. Thanking all who accompanied me with prayer and continue to be near me with their spiritual support, I invoke the Mother of the Redeemer so that my visit to places in which two thousand years ago the Word of God "pitched his tent" among men may redound to the benefit of the whole Church and the entire world.

The Pope's Spiritual Preparation for the Holy Land

While still at the Vatican, John Paul prepared for his Jubilee Pilgrimage with a week's Spiritual Exercises, praying and meditating on reflections prepared for him by Vietnamese Archbishop François Xavier Nguyên Van Thuân.

The archbishop, president of the Pontifical Council for Justice and Peace, used the disciples on the road to Emmaus as a theme of his retreat, saying, "The peace Jesus announces to his disciples is also love. The heart reconciles in love, it is unified, and it reaches that peace for which we have been created and which is our end....The incident of Emmaus reminds all of us of a joyful reality of the Christian experience: the perennial presence of the resurrected Christ in the Church. [Therefore] let us constantly return to Jerusalem...to the sources, to the Church's center."

After thanking the archbishop for the week's retreat in the Vatican, which was especially significant before the Holy Land journey, the pope also said, "The Great Jubilee we are celebrating takes us step by step to go profoundly into the reasons for our Christian hope, which demands and fosters increasing trust in God and an ever more generous opening to brothers."

6. Discourse upon Arrival in Jordan

March 20, 2000

Your Majesties,
Members of the Government,

1. In a spirit of profound respect and friendship, I offer greetings to all who live in the Hashemite Kingdom of Jordan: the members of the Catholic Church and the other Christian Churches, the Muslim people whom we followers of Jesus Christ hold in high esteem, and all men and women of good will.

My visit to your country and the entire journey that I am beginning today is part of the religious Jubilee Pilgrimage that I am making to commemorate the two-thousandth anniversary of the birth of Jesus Christ. From the beginning of my ministry as Bishop of Rome, I have had a great desire to mark this event by praying in some of the places linked to salvation history—places that speak to us of that moment's long preparation through biblical times, places where our Lord Jesus Christ actually lived, or which are connected with his work of redemption. I have already been to Egypt and Mount Sinai, where God revealed his name to Moses and entrusted to him the tablets of the Law of the covenant.

2. Today I am in Jordan, a land familiar to me from the Holy Scriptures: a land sanctified by the presence of Jesus himself, by the presence of Moses, Elijah, and John the Baptist, and of saints and martyrs of the early Church. Yours is a land noted for its hospitality and openness to all.

These are qualities of the Jordanian people, which I have experienced many times in conversations with the late King Hussein, and which were confirmed anew in my meeting with Your Majesty at the Vatican in September last year.

Your Majesty, I know how deeply concerned you are for peace in your own land and in the entire region, and how important it is to you that all Jordanians—Muslims and Christians—should consider themselves as one people and one family. In this area of the world there are grave and urgent issues of justice, of the rights of peoples and nations, which have to be resolved for the good of all concerned and as a condition for lasting peace. No matter how difficult, no matter how long, the process of seeking peace must continue. Without peace, there can be no authentic development for this region, no better life for its peoples, no brighter future for its children. That is why Jordan's proven commitment to securing the conditions necessary for peace is so important and praiseworthy.

Building a future of peace requires an ever more mature understanding and ever more practical cooperation among the peoples who acknowledge the one true, indivisible God, the Creator of all that exists. The three historical monotheistic religions count peace, goodness, and respect for the human person among their highest values. I earnestly hope that my visit will strengthen the already-fruitful Christian-Muslim dialogue that is being conducted in Jordan, particularly through the Royal Interfaith Institute.

3. The Catholic Church, without forgetting that her primary mission is a spiritual one, is always eager to coop-

erate with individual nations and people of goodwill in promoting and advancing the dignity of the human person. She does this particularly in her schools and education programs, and through her charitable and social institutions. Your noble tradition of respect for all religions guarantees the religious freedom that makes this possible, and that is in fact a fundamental human right. When this is so, all citizens feel themselves equal, and each one, inspired by his [or her] own spiritual convictions, can contribute to the building up of society as the shared home of all.

4. The warm invitation which Your Majesties, the Government, and the people of Jordan have extended to me is an expression of our common hope for a new era of peace and development in this region. I am truly grateful, and with deep appreciation of your kindness I assure you of my prayers for you, for all the Jordanian people, for the displaced people in your midst, and for the young people who make up such a large part of the population.

May Almighty God grant Your Majesties happiness and long life!

May he bless Jordan with prosperity and peace!

7. Prayer at Wadi Al-Kharrar, Jordan

March 21, 2000

In the Gospel of Saint Luke we read that "the word of God came to John the son of Zechariah in the wilderness; and he went into all the region about the Jordan, preaching a baptism of repentance for the forgiveness of sins" (3:2–3). Here, at the River Jordan, where both banks are visited by hosts of pilgrims honoring the Baptism of the Lord, I too lift up my heart in prayer:

Glory to you, O Father, God of Abraham, Isaac, and Jacob! You sent your servants the prophets to speak your word of faithful love and call your people to repentance. On the banks of the River Jordan, you raised up John the Baptist, a voice crying in the wilderness, sent through all the region of the Jordan to prepare the way of the Lord, to herald the coming of Jesus.

Glory to you, O Christ, Son of God! To the waters of the Jordan you came to be baptized by the hand of John. Upon you the Spirit descended as a dove. Above you the heavens opened, and the voice of the Father was heard: "This is my Son, the Beloved!" From the river blessed by your presence you went forth to baptize not only with water but with fire and the Holy Spirit.

Glory to you, O Holy Spirit, Lord and Giver of life! By your power, the Church is baptized, going down with Christ into death and rising with him to new life. By your power, we are set free from sin to become the children of God, the glorious Body of Christ. By your power, all fear is vanquished, and the Gospel of love is preached in every corner of the earth, to the glory of God, the Father, the Son, and the Holy Spirit, to whom be all praise in this Jubilee year and in every age to come. Amen.

8. Discourse upon Arrival in Israel

March 21, 2000

Dear President Weizman,
Dear Israeli Friends,
Your Excellencies, Ladies, and Gentlemen,

1. Yesterday, from the heights of Mount Nebo I looked across the Jordan Valley to this blessed land. Today, it is with profound emotion that I set foot in the land where God chose to "pitch his tent" (John 1:14; cf. Exod 40:34–35; 1 Kgs 8:10–13), and made it possible for man to encounter him more directly.

In this year of the two-thousandth anniversary of the birth of Jesus Christ, it has been my strong personal desire to come here and to pray in the most important places which, from ancient times, have seen God's interventions, the wonders he has done. "You are the God who works wonders. You showed your power among the peoples" (Ps 77:15).

Mr. President, I thank you for your warm welcome, and in your person I greet all the people of the State of Israel.

2. My visit is both a personal pilgrimage and the spiritual journey of the Bishop of Rome to the origins of our faith in "the God of Abraham, of Isaac, and of Jacob" (Exod 3:15). It is part of a larger pilgrimage of prayer and thanksgiving that led me first to Sinai, the Mountain of the Covenant, the place of the decisive revelation that shaped the subsequent history of salvation. Now I shall have the privilege of visiting some of the places more

closely connected with the life, death, and resurrection of Jesus Christ. Along every step of the way I am moved by a vivid sense of God who has gone before us and leads us on, who wants us to honor him in spirit and in truth, to acknowledge the differences between us, but also to recognize in every human being the image and likeness of the One Creator of heaven and earth.

3. Mr. President, you are known as a man of peace and a peacemaker. We all know how urgent is the need for peace and justice, not for Israel alone but for the entire region. Many things have changed in relations between the Holy See and the State of Israel since my predecessor Pope Paul VI came here in 1964. The establishment of diplomatic relations between us in 1994 set a seal on efforts to open an era of dialogue on questions of common interest concerning religious freedom, relations between Church and State, and more generally, relations between Christians and Jews. On another level, world opinion follows with close attention the peace process, which finds all the peoples of the region involved in the difficult search for a lasting peace with justice for all. With new-found openness toward one another, Christians and Jews together must make courageous efforts to remove all forms of prejudice. We must strive always and everywhere to present the true face of the Jews and of Judaism, as likewise of Christians and of Christianity, and this at every level of attitude, teaching, and communication (Address to the Jewish Community of Rome, April 13, 1986, 5).

4. My journey therefore is a pilgrimage, in a spirit of humble gratitude and hope, to the origins of our religious

history. It is a tribute to the three religious traditions that coexist in this land. For a long time I have looked forward to meeting the faithful of the Catholic communities in their rich variety, and the members of the various Christian Churches and communities present in the Holy Land. I pray that my visit will serve to encourage an increase of interreligious dialogue that will lead Jews, Christians, and Muslims to seek in their respective beliefs, and in the universal brotherhood that unites all the members of the human family, the motivation and the perseverance to work for the peace and justice that the peoples of the Holy Land do not yet have, and for which they yearn so deeply. The psalmist reminds us that peace is God's gift: "I will hear what the Lord God has to say, a voice that speaks of peace, peace for his people and his friends, and those who turn to him in their hearts" (Ps 85:8).

May peace be God's gift to the land he chose as his own!

9. Address upon Arrival in Palestinian Territory

March 22, 2000

Dear Chairman Arafat,
Your Excellencies,
Dear Palestinian Friends,

1. "Here Christ was born of the Virgin Mary": these words, inscribed over the place where, according to tradition, Jesus was born, are the reason for the Great Jubilee

of the year 2000. They are the reason for my coming to Bethlehem today. They are the source of the joy, the hope, the goodwill that, for two millennia, have filled countless human hearts at the very sound of the name "Bethlehem."

People everywhere turn to this unique corner of the earth with a hope that transcends all conflicts and difficulties. Bethlehem—where the choir of angels sang: "Glory to God in the highest, and on earth peace among men" (Luke 2:14)—stands out, in every place and in every age, as the promise of God's gift of peace. The message of Bethlehem is the Good News of reconciliation among men, of peace at every level of relations between individuals and nations. Bethlehem is a universal crossroads where all peoples can meet to build together a world worthy of our human dignity and destiny. The recently inaugurated Museum of the Nativity shows how the celebration of Christ's birth has become a part of the culture and art of peoples in all parts of the world.

2. Mr. Arafat, as I thank you for the warm welcome you have given me in the name of the Palestinian Authority and people, I express all my happiness at being here today. How can I fail to pray that the divine gift of peace will become more and more a reality for all who live in this land, uniquely marked by God's interventions? Peace for the Palestinian people! Peace for all the peoples of the region! No one can ignore how much the Palestinian people have had to suffer in recent decades. Your torment is before the eyes of the world. And it has gone on too long.

The Holy See has always recognized that the Palestinian people have the natural right to a homeland, and the right to be able to live in peace and tranquility with the other peoples of this area (Apostolic Letter *Redemptionis Anno,* April 20, 1984). In the international forum, my predecessors and I have repeatedly proclaimed that there would be no end to the sad conflict in the Holy Land without stable guarantees for the rights of all the peoples involved, on the basis of international law and the relevant United Nations resolutions and declarations.

We must all continue to work and pray for the success of every genuine effort to bring peace to this land. Only with a just and lasting peace—not imposed but secured through negotiation—will legitimate Palestinian aspirations be fulfilled. Only then will the Holy Land see the possibility of a bright new future, no longer dissipated by rivalry and conflict, but firmly based on understanding and cooperation for the good of all. The outcome depends greatly on the courageous readiness of those responsible for the destiny of this part of the world to move to new attitudes of compromise and compliance with the demands of justice.

3. Dear Friends, I am fully aware of the great challenges facing the Palestinian Authority and people in every field of economic and cultural development. In a particular way my prayers are with those Palestinians— Muslim and Christian—who are still without a home of their own, their proper place in society, and the possibility of a normal working life. My hope is that my visit today to the Dheisheh Refugee Camp will serve to remind the

international community that decisive action is needed to improve the situation of the Palestinian people. I was particularly pleased at the unanimous acceptance by the United Nations of the Resolution on Bethlehem 2000, which commits the international community to help in developing this area and in improving conditions of peace and reconciliation in one of the most cherished and significant places on earth.

The promise of peace made at Bethlehem will become a reality for the world only when the dignity and rights of all human beings made in the image of God (Gen 1:26) are acknowledged and respected.

Today and always the Palestinian people are in my prayers to the One who holds the destiny of the world in his hands. May the Most High God enlighten, sustain, and guide in the path of peace the whole Palestinian people!

10. Homily in Manger Square, Bethlehem

March 22, 2000

> "To us a Child is born, to us a Son is given...and his name will be called 'Wonderful Counselor, Mighty God...Prince of Peace.'" (Isa 9:6)

Your Beatitude, Brother Bishops and Priests,
Dear Brothers and Sisters,

1. The words of the prophet Isaiah foreshadow the Savior's coming into the world. And it was here in Bethlehem that the great promise was fulfilled. For two

thousand years, generation after generation of Christians has pronounced the name of Bethlehem with deep emotion and joyful gratitude. Like the shepherds and the wise men, we too have come to find the Child, "wrapped in swaddling clothes and lying in a manger" (Luke 2:12). Like so many pilgrims before us, we kneel in wonder and adoration before the ineffable mystery that was accomplished here.

On the first Christmas of my ministry as Successor of the Apostle Peter, I mentioned publicly the great desire I had to celebrate the beginning of my pontificate in Bethlehem at the cave of the Nativity (Homily at Midnight Mass, December 24, 1978, No. 3). That was not possible then, and has not been possible until now. But today, how can I fail to praise the God of all mercies, whose ways are mysterious and whose love knows no end, for bringing me, in this year of the Great Jubilee, to the place of the Savior's birth? Bethlehem is the heart of my Jubilee Pilgrimage. The paths that I have taken lead me to this place and to the mystery that it proclaims.

I thank Patriarch Michel Sabbah for his kind words of welcome and I cordially embrace all the members of the Assembly of the Catholic Ordinaries of the Holy Land. Significant is the presence, in the place that saw the birth of the Son of God in the flesh, of many of the Eastern Catholic communities that form the rich mosaic of our catholicity. With affection in the Lord, I greet the representatives of the Orthodox Churches and of the ecclesial communities present in the Holy Land.

I am grateful to the officials of the Palestinian Authority who are taking part in our celebration and joining us in praying for the well-being of the Palestinian people.

2. "Do not be afraid! Listen, I bring you news of great joy, a joy to be shared by the whole people. Today in the town of David a Savior has been born to you: he is Christ the Lord" (Luke 2:10–11).

The joy announced by the angel is not a thing of the past. It is a joy of today—the eternal today of God's salvation that embraces all time, past, present, and future. At the dawn of the new millennium, we are called to see more clearly that time has meaning because here Eternity entered history and remains with us forever. The words of the Venerable Bede express the idea clearly: "Still today, and every day until the end of the ages, the Lord will be continually conceived in Nazareth and born in Bethlehem" (In *Ev. S. Lucae*, 2: PL 92, 330). Because it is always Christmas in Bethlehem, every day is Christmas in the hearts of Christians. And every day we are called to proclaim the message of Bethlehem to the world—"good news of great joy": the Eternal Word, "God from God, Light from Light," has become flesh and has made his dwelling among us (John 1:14).

The newborn Child, defenseless and totally dependent on the care of Mary and Joseph, entrusted to their love, is the world's entire wealth. He is our all! In this Child—the Son who is given to us—we find rest for our souls and the true bread that never fails—the Eucharistic Bread foreshadowed even in the name of this town: Beth-lehem, the house of bread. God lies hidden in the Child; divinity lies hidden in the Bread of Life. *Adoro te devote latens Deitas! Quae sub his figuris vere latitas!*

3. The great mystery of divine self-emptying, the work of our redemption unfolding in weakness: this is no easy truth. The Savior was born in the night—in the darkness, in the silence and poverty of the cave of Bethlehem. "The people who walked in darkness have seen a great light: on those who live in a land of deep shadow a light has shone," declares the prophet Isaiah (9:2). This is a place that has known "the yoke" and "the rod" of oppression. How often has the cry of innocents been heard in these streets? Even the great church built over the Savior's birthplace stands like a fortress battered by the strife of the ages. The crib of Jesus lies always in the shadow of the cross. The silence and poverty of the birth in Bethlehem are one with the darkness and pain of the death on Calvary. The crib and the cross are the same mystery of redemptive love; the body which Mary laid in the manger is the same body offered up on the cross.

4. Where then is the dominion of the "Wonderful Counselor, Mighty God, and Prince of Peace" of which the prophet Isaiah speaks? What is the power to which Jesus himself refers when he says: "All power has been given to me in heaven and on earth" (Matt 28:18)? Christ's kingdom is "not of this world" (John 18:36). His kingdom is not the play of force and wealth and conquest that appears to shape our human history. It is rather the power to vanquish the Evil One, the ultimate victory over sin and death. It is the power to heal the wounds that disfigure the image of the Creator in his creatures. Christ's is

the power to transform our weak nature and make us capable, through the grace of the Holy Spirit, of peace with one another and communion with God himself. "To all who received him, who believed in his name, he gave power to become children of God" (John 1:12). This is the message of Bethlehem today and forever. This is the extraordinary gift that the Prince of Peace brought into the world two thousand years ago.

5. In that peace, I greet all the Palestinian people, aware as I am that this is an especially important time in your history. I pray that the recently concluded pastoral synod in which all the Catholic Churches took part will encourage you and strengthen among you the bonds of unity and peace. In this way you will bear ever more effective witness to the faith, building up the Church and serving the common good. I offer the holy kiss to the Christians of the other Churches and ecclesial communities. I greet the Muslim community of Bethlehem and pray for a new era of understanding and cooperation among all the peoples of the Holy Land.

Today we look back to one moment two thousand years ago, but in spirit we embrace all time. We gather in one place, but we encompass the whole earth. We celebrate one newborn Child, but we embrace all men and women everywhere. Today from Manger Square, we cry out to every time and place, and to every person, "Peace be with you! Do not be afraid!" These words resound through the pages of Scripture. They are divine words, spoken by Jesus himself after he rose from the dead: "Do not be afraid!" (Matt 28:10). They are the words of the

Church to you today. Do not be afraid to preserve your Christian presence and heritage in the very place where the Savior was born. In the cave of Bethlehem, to use the words of Saint Paul in today's second reading, "God's grace has been revealed" (Titus 2:11). In the Child who is born, the world has received "the mercy promised to our fathers, to Abraham and his descendants forever" (Luke 1:54–55). Dazzled by the mystery of the Eternal Word made flesh, we leave all fear behind and we become like the angels, glorifying God who gives the world such gifts. With the heavenly choir, we "sing a new song" (Ps 96:1): "Glory to God in the highest heaven, and peace on earth to those whom he loves" (Luke 2:14).

O Child of Bethlehem, Son of Mary and Son of God, Lord of All Time and Prince of Peace, "the same yesterday, today, and for ever" (Heb 13:8): as we set forth into the new millennium, heal all our wounds, strengthen our steps, open our hearts and minds to "the loving kindness of the heart of our God who visits us like the dawn from on high" (Luke 1:78). Amen.

11. Visit to the Palestinian Refugee Camp of Dheisheh, Palestinian Territory

March 22, 2000

Dear Friends,
Dear Brother and Sister Refugees,

1. It is important to me that my pilgrimage to the birthplace of Jesus Christ, on this the two-thousandth

anniversary of that extraordinary event, includes this visit to Dheisheh. It is deeply significant that here, close to Bethlehem, I am meeting you, refugees and displaced persons, and representatives of the organizations and agencies involved in a true mission of mercy. Throughout my pontificate I have felt close to the Palestinian people in their sufferings.

I greet each one of you, and I hope and pray that my visit will bring some comfort in your difficult situation. Please God it will help to draw attention to your continuing plight. You have been deprived of many things that represent basic needs of the human person: proper housing, health care, education, and work. Above all you bear the sad memory of what you were forced to leave behind, not just material possessions, but your freedom, the closeness of relatives, and the familiar surroundings and cultural traditions that nourished your personal and family life. It is true that much is being done here in Dheisheh and in other camps to respond to your needs, especially through the United Nations Relief and Works Agency. I am particularly pleased at the effectiveness of the presence of the Pontifical Mission for Palestine and many other Catholic organizations. But there is still much to be done.

2. The degrading conditions in which refugees often have to live; the continuation over long periods of situations that are barely tolerable in emergencies or for a brief time of transit; the fact that displaced persons are obliged to remain for years in settlement camps: these are the measure of the urgent need for a just solution to the

underlying causes of the problem. Only a resolute effort on the part of leaders in the Middle East and in the international community as a whole—inspired by a higher vision of politics as service of the common good—can remove the causes of your present situation. My appeal is for greater international solidarity and the political will to meet this challenge. I plead with all who are sincerely working for justice and peace not to lose heart. I appeal to political leaders to implement agreements already arrived at, and to go forward toward the peace for which all reasonable men and women yearn, to the justice to which they have an inalienable right.

3. Dear young people, continue to strive through education to take your rightful place in society, despite the difficulties and handicaps that you have to face because of your refugee status. The Catholic Church is particularly happy to serve the noble cause of education through the extremely valuable work of Bethlehem University, founded as a sequel to the visit of my predecessor Pope Paul VI in 1964.

Dear refugees, do not think that your present condition makes you any less important in God's eyes!

Never forget your dignity as his children! Here at Bethlehem the Divine Child was laid in a manger in a stable; shepherds from nearby fields who were your ancestors were the first to receive the heavenly message of peace and hope for the world. God's design was fulfilled in the midst of humility and poverty.

Dear aid workers and volunteers, believe in the task that you are fulfilling! Genuine and practical solidarity with those in need is not a favor conceded, it is a demand of our shared humanity and a recognition of the dignity of every human being.

Let us all turn with confidence to the Lord, asking him to inspire those in a position of responsibility to promote justice, security, and peace, without delay and in an eminently practical way.

The Church, through her social and charitable organizations, will continue to be at your side and to plead your cause before the world. God bless you all!

12. Address during Courtesy Visit to Yasser Arafat

March 22, 2000

Your Excellency,

I am happy to have this opportunity to thank you again, and to return the visits that you have made to me in the Vatican. I thank you for your warm welcome. This is an important moment in the search for peace in this region. Much has been achieved, but there is still much to be done if all the peoples of the region are to live in harmony based upon respect for the rights and dignity of all.

Our meeting today makes clear the commitment of the Catholic Church to work unceasingly for peace in the Middle East as a partner of all peoples. The Church understands the aspirations of the different peoples and insists that dialogue is the only way to make those aspirations a reality rather than a dream. I am thankful for the recognition you have given me here today. I know that you too are convinced that only patient and courageous dialogue will open the way to the future that your people rightly desire.

Entrusting this great challenge to Almighty God, I invoke upon you, upon your family and the Palestinian people, the abundant blessings of heaven.

13. Homily in the Upper Room, Jerusalem

March 23, 2000

1. "This is my Body."

Gathered in the Upper Room, we have listened to the Gospel account of the Last Supper. We have heard words that emerge from the depths of the mystery of the Incarnation of the Son of God. Jesus takes bread, blesses and breaks it, then gives it to his disciples, saying: "This is my Body."

God's covenant with his people is about to culminate in the sacrifice of his Son, the Eternal Word made flesh. The ancient prophecies are about to be fulfilled: "Sacrifices and offerings you desired not, but a body you have prepared for me....Lo, I have come to do your will, O God" (Heb 10:5, 7). In the Incarnation, the Son of God, of one being with the Father, became Man and received a body from the Virgin Mary. And now, on the night before his death, he says to his disciples: "This is my Body, which will be given up for you."

It is with deep emotion that we listen once more to these words spoken here in this Upper Room two thousand years ago. Since then they have been repeated, generation after generation, by those who share in the priesthood of Christ through the sacrament of Holy Orders. In this way, Christ himself constantly says these words anew, through the voice of his priests in every corner of the world.

2. "This is the cup of my Blood, the Blood of the new and everlasting covenant; it will be shed for you and for all, for the forgiveness of sins. Do this in memory of me."

In obedience to Christ's command, the Church repeats these words each day in the celebration of the Eucharist, words which rise from the depths of the mystery of the Redemption. At the celebration of the Passover meal in the Upper Room, Jesus took the cup filled with wine, blessed it, and gave it to his disciples. This was part of the Passover rite of the Old Testament. But Christ, the Priest of the new and eternal covenant, used these words to proclaim the saving mystery of his passion and death.

Under the appearances of bread and wine he instituted the sacramental signs of the Sacrifice of his Body and Blood.

"By your cross and resurrection, you have set us free. You are the Savior of the world." At every Holy Mass, we proclaim this "mystery of faith," which for two millennia has nourished and sustained the Church as she makes her pilgrim way amid the persecutions of the world and the consolations of God, proclaiming the cross and death of the Lord until he comes (*Lumen Gentium*, 8). In a sense, Peter and the apostles, in the person of their successors, have come back today to the Upper Room, to profess the unchanging faith of the Church: "Christ has died, Christ is risen, Christ will come again."

3. In fact, the first reading of today's liturgy leads us back to the life of the first Christian community. The disciples "devoted themselves to the apostles' teaching and fellowship, to the breaking of bread and the prayers" (Acts 2:42).

Fractio panis. The Eucharist is both a banquet of communion in the new and everlasting covenant, and the sacrifice which makes present the saving power of the cross. And from the very beginning the Eucharistic mystery has always been linked to the teaching and fellowship of the apostles and to the proclamation of God's word, spoken first through the prophets and now, once and for all, in Jesus Christ (Heb 1:1–2). Wherever the words "This is my Body" and the invocation of the Holy Spirit are pronounced, the Church is strengthened in the faith of the apostles and in the unity that has the Holy Spirit as its origin and bond.

4. Saint Paul, the Apostle of the Nations, saw clearly that the Eucharist, as our sharing in the Body and Blood of Christ, is also a mystery of spiritual communion in the Church. "We, many though we are, are one body, for we all partake of the same bread" (1 Cor 10:17). In the Eucharist, Christ the Good Shepherd, who gave his life for the sheep, remains present in his Church. What is the Eucharist, if not the sacramental presence of Christ in all who share in the one bread and the one cup? This presence is the Church's greatest wealth. Through the Eucharist, Christ builds up the Church. The hands which

broke bread for the disciples at the Last Supper were to be stretched out on the cross in order to gather all people to himself in the eternal Kingdom of his Father. Through the celebration of the Eucharist, he never ceases to draw men and women to be effective members of his Body.

5. "Christ has died, Christ is risen, Christ will come again."

This is the "mystery of faith" which we proclaim in every celebration of the Eucharist. Jesus Christ, the Priest of the new and eternal covenant, has redeemed the world by his Blood. Risen from the dead, he has gone to prepare a place for us in his Father's house. In the Spirit who has made us God's beloved children, in the unity of the Body of Christ, we await his return with joyful hope.

This year of the Great Jubilee is a special opportunity for priests to grow in appreciation of the mystery which they celebrate at the altar. For that reason I wish to sign this year's "Letter to Priests for Holy Thursday" here in the Upper Room, where the one priesthood of Jesus Christ, in which we all share, was instituted.

Celebrating this Eucharist in the Upper Room in Jerusalem, we are united with the Church of every time and place. United with the Head, we are in communion with Peter and the apostles and their successors down the ages. In union with Mary, the saints and martyrs, and all the baptized who have lived in the grace of the Holy Spirit, we cry out: *Marana tha*! "Come, Lord Jesus!" (Rev 22:20).

Bring us, and all your chosen ones, to the fullness of grace in your eternal Kingdom. Amen.

14. Visit to the Two Chief Rabbis of Israel, Jerusalem

March 23, 2000

Very Reverend Chief Rabbis,

It is with deep respect that I visit you here today and thank you for receiving me at Hechal Shlomo. Truly this is a uniquely significant meeting which—I hope and pray—will lead to increasing contacts between Christians and Jews, aimed at achieving an ever-deeper understanding of the historical and theological relationship between our respective religious heritages.

Personally, I have always wanted to be counted among those who work, on both sides, to overcome old prejudices and to secure ever wider and fuller recognition of the spiritual patrimony shared by Jews and Christians. I repeat what I said on the occasion of my visit to the Jewish community in Rome, that we Christians recognize that the Jewish religious heritage is intrinsic to our own faith: "You are our elder brothers" (Address at the Synagogue of Rome, April 13, 1986, 4). We hope that the Jewish people will acknowledge that the Church utterly condemns anti-Semitism and every form of racism as being altogether opposed to the principles of Christianity. We must work together to build a future in which there will be no more anti-Judaism among Christians or anti-Christian sentiment among Jews.

There is much that we have in common. There is so much that we can do together for peace, for justice, for a more human and fraternal world. May the Lord of heaven and earth lead us to a new and fruitful era of mutual respect and cooperation, for the benefit of all! Thank you.

15. Courtesy Visit to the President of Israel

March 23, 2000

Mr. President,
Government Ministers,
Members of the Knesset,
Your Excellencies,

I am most grateful, Mr. President, for the welcome you have given me to Israel. To this meeting we both bring long histories. You represent Jewish memory, reaching beyond the recent history of this land to your people's unique journey through the centuries and millennia. I come as one whose Christian memory reaches back through the two thousand years since the birth of Jesus in this very land.

History, as the ancients held, is the *Magistra vitae,* a teacher of how to live. This is why we must be determined to heal the wounds of the past, so that they may never be opened again. We must work for a new era of reconciliation and peace between Jews and Christians. My visit is a pledge that the Catholic Church will do everything possible to ensure that this is not just a dream but a reality. We know that real peace in the Middle East will come only as a result of mutual understanding and respect between all the peoples of the region: Jews, Christians, and Muslims. In this perspective, my pilgrimage is a journey of hope:

the hope that the twenty-first century will lead to a new solidarity among the peoples of the world, in the conviction that development, justice, and peace will not be attained unless they are attained for all.

Building a brighter future for the human family is a task which concerns us all. That is why I am pleased to greet you—government ministers, members of the Knesset, and diplomatic representatives of many countries—who must make and implement decisions that affect the lives of people. It is my fervent hope that a genuine desire for peace will inspire your every decision. With that as my prayer, I invoke abundant divine blessings upon you, Mr. President, upon your country, and upon all of you who have honored me with your presence. Thank you.

Emotional Meeting Between the Pope and His Childhood Jewish Friend

At Yad Vashem, the pope was reunited with his childhood friend Yossef Bainenstock, whom he had not seen for fifty years. Separated first by their different paths growing up and later by the Second World War, the two had been classmates and close friends. Their embrace was emotional, deeply moving both them and those who witnessed it.

Bainenstock spoke to the pope in Polish and called him by his nickname, "Lolek." They reminisced about their many soccer games, skiing trips, and classes together. Bainenstock remembered the brilliance of his young friend, how Lolek would know the answer before the teacher had finished asking the question. Bainenstock also confessed that the pope had generously let him copy from his work and so he was able to pass the exams.

Bainenstock later went on to rabbinical school and became a watchmaker like his father, while Lolek went off to Cracow to study. Bainenstock's watchmaking skills were much prized in the concentration camp and probably saved his life.

At their reunion, John Paul asked about Bainenstock's family, but most had died at Auschwitz or Dachau. After the war, Bainenstock left Germany for Israel, living at first on a kibbutz. He knew his old friend had gone on to become pope and for many years had considered asking for an audience with him at the Vatican. But Bainenstock had also hoped that his old "playmate," as he called the pope, would eventually come to Israel.

"I was a Jew and he a Christian, but we saw nothing strange in our friendship," Bainenstock recalled.

16. Visit to the Yad Vashem Holocaust Memorial, Jerusalem

March 23, 2000

The words of the ancient psalm rise from our hearts:

I have become like a broken vessel.
I hear the whispering of many—terror on every
    side!—

as they scheme together against me, as they plot to
  take my life.
But I trust in you, O Lord;
I say, "You are my God." (Ps 31:12–15)

1. In this place of memories, the mind and heart and
soul feel an extreme need for silence. Silence in which to
remember. Silence in which to try to make some sense of
the memories that come flooding back. Silence because
there are no words strong enough to deplore the terrible
tragedy of the *Shoah*.

My own personal memories are of all that happened
when the Nazis occupied Poland during the War. I
remember my Jewish friends and neighbors, some of
whom perished, while others survived. I have come to Yad
Vashem to pay homage to the millions of Jewish people
who, stripped of everything, especially of their human
dignity, were murdered in the Holocaust. More than half
a century has passed, but the memories remain.

Here, as at Auschwitz and many other places in
Europe, we are overcome by the echo of the heart-rending
laments of so many. Men, women, and children cry out to
us from the depths of the horror that they knew. How can
we fail to heed their cry? No one can forget or ignore what
happened. No one can diminish its scale.

2. We wish to remember. But we wish to remember for
a purpose, namely to ensure that never again will evil prevail, as it did for the millions of innocent victims of Nazism.

How could man have such utter contempt for man?
Because he had reached the point of contempt for God.

Only a godless ideology could plan and carry out the extermination of a whole people.

The honor given to the "just gentiles" by the State of Israel at Yad Vashem for having acted heroically to save Jews, sometimes to the point of giving their own lives, is a recognition that not even in the darkest hour is every light extinguished. That is why the Psalms, and the entire Bible, though well aware of the human capacity for evil, also proclaim that evil will not have the last word. Out of the depths of pain and sorrow, the believer's heart cries out: "I trust in you, O Lord; I say, 'You are my God'" (Ps 31:14).

3. Jews and Christians share an immense spiritual patrimony, flowing from God's self-revelation. Our religious teachings and our spiritual experience demand that we overcome evil with good. We remember, but not with any desire for vengeance or as an incentive to hatred. For us, to remember is to pray for peace and justice, and to commit ourselves to their cause. Only a world at peace, with justice for all, can avoid repeating the mistakes and terrible crimes of the past.

As bishop of Rome and successor of the apostle Peter, I assure the Jewish people that the Catholic Church, motivated by the Gospel law of truth and love and by no political considerations, is deeply saddened by the hatred, acts of persecution, and displays of anti-Semitism directed against the Jews by Christians at any time and in any place. The Church rejects racism in any form as a denial of the image of the Creator inherent in every human being (Gen 1:26).

4. In this place of solemn remembrance, I fervently pray that our sorrow for the tragedy that the Jewish

people suffered in the twentieth century will lead to a new relationship between Christians and Jews. Let us build a new future in which there will be no more anti-Jewish feeling among Christians or anti-Christian feeling among Jews, but rather the mutual respect required of those who adore the one Creator and Lord, and look to Abraham as our common father in faith (*We Remember*, V).

The world must heed the warning that comes to us from the victims of the Holocaust and from the testimony of the survivors. Here at Yad Vashem the memory lives on, and burns itself onto our souls. It makes us cry out: "I hear the whispering of many—terror on every side!—But I trust in you, O Lord; I say, 'You are my God'" (Ps 31:13–15).

Letter from Polish Mother Moves John Paul ll

One of many emotionally charged moments at Yad Vashem's ceremony at the Holocaust Memorial was the reading of a 1943 letter, written by one Polish mother to another. The letter writer, a Jewish woman, was being sent to a camp and was entrusting her son to her friend, hoping he would thus escape her fate. He was eventually captured, however, and both he and his mother died in Auschwitz.

The pope was deeply moved by the mother's plea that the friend care for the boy like her own, that she keep him warm as he was weak and sickly.

"Dear Bronia," the mother wrote, "do everything possible for him, I will be grateful to you until my dying day. [My son] is very intelligent and has a very good heart. I am sure he will love you. Every day I pray to God, from the depth of my suffering that you, on the contrary, will have a happy future, and will not have to be separated from your children, so that you can love them and take care of them. Can you understand my torture?

"Bronia, this letter is a cry from the heart. Michael must eat, become strong, be able to withstand sufferings. Please, it is necessary to dress him in warm clothes, that he wear socks. I cannot go on writing. Even my tears have dried up. May God protect you both. Genya."

17. Interreligious Meeting at Notre Dame Pontifical Institute, Jerusalem

March 23, 2000

Distinguished Jewish, Christian,
and Muslim Representatives

1. In this year of the two-thousandth anniversary of the birth of Jesus Christ, I am truly happy to be able to fulfill my long-cherished wish to make a journey through the geography of salvation history. I am deeply moved as I follow in the footsteps of the countless pilgrims who before me have prayed in the holy places connected with God's interventions. I am fully conscious that this land is holy to Jews, Christians, and Muslims. Therefore, my visit would have been incomplete without this meeting with you, distinguished religious leaders. Thank you for the support which your presence here this evening gives to

the hope and conviction of so many people that we are indeed entering a new era of interreligious dialogue. We are conscious that closer ties among all believers are a necessary and urgent condition for securing a more just and peaceful world.

For all of us, Jerusalem, as its name indicates, is the "City of Peace." Perhaps no other place in the world communicates the sense of transcendence and divine election that we perceive in her stones and monuments, and in the witness of the three religions living side by side within her walls. Not everything has been or will be easy in this coexistence. But we must find in our respective religious traditions the wisdom and the superior motivation to ensure the triumph of mutual understanding and cordial respect.

2. We all agree that religion must be genuinely centered on God, and that our first religious duty is adoration, praise, and thanksgiving. The opening sura of the Qur'ân makes this clear: "Praise be to God, the Lord of the Universe" (Qur'ân, 1:1). In the inspired songs of the Bible we hear this universal call: "Let everything that breathes give praise to the Lord! Alleluia!" (Ps 150:6). And in the Gospel we read that when Jesus was born the angels sang: "Glory to God in the highest heaven" (Luke 2:14). In our times, when many are tempted to run their affairs without any reference to God, the call to acknowledge the Creator of the universe and the Lord of history is essential in ensuring the well-being of individuals and the proper development of society.

3. If it is authentic, devotion to God necessarily involves attention to our fellow human beings. As mem-

bers of the one human family and as God's beloved children, we have duties toward one another that, as believers, we cannot ignore. One of the first disciples of Jesus wrote: "If any one says, 'I love God,' and hates his brother, he is a liar; for he who does not love his brother whom he has seen, cannot love God whom he has not seen" (1 John 4:20). Love of our brothers and sisters involves an attitude of respect and compassion, gestures of solidarity, cooperation in service to the common good. Thus, concern for justice and peace does not lie outside the field of religion but is actually one of its essential elements.

In the Christian view it is not for religious leaders to propose technical formulas for the solution of social, economic, and political problems. Theirs is, above all, the task of teaching the truths of faith and right conduct, the task of helping people—including those with responsibility in public life—to be aware of their duties and to fulfill them. As religious leaders, we help people to live integrated lives, to harmonize the vertical dimension of their relationship with God with the horizontal dimension of service to their neighbor.

4. Each of our religions knows, in some form or another, the Golden Rule: "Do unto others as you would have them do unto you." Precious as this rule is as a guide, true love of neighbor goes much further. It is based on the conviction that when we love our neighbor we are showing love for God, and when we hurt our neighbor we offend God. This means that religion is the enemy of exclusion and discrimination, of hatred and rivalry, of violence and conflict. Religion is not, and must not

become, an excuse for violence, particularly when religious identity coincides with cultural and ethnic identity. Religion and peace go together! Religious belief and practice cannot be separated from the defense of the image of God in every human being.

Drawing upon the riches of our respective religious traditions, we must spread awareness that today's problems will not be solved if we remain ignorant of one another and isolated from one another. We are all aware of past misunderstandings and conflicts, and these still weigh heavily upon relationships between Jews, Christians, and Muslims. We must do all we can to turn awareness of past offences and sins into a firm resolve to build a new future in which there will be nothing but respectful and fruitful cooperation between us.

The Catholic Church wishes to pursue a sincere and fruitful interreligious dialogue with the members of the Jewish faith and the followers of Islam. Such a dialogue is not an attempt to impose our views upon others. What it demands of all of us is that, holding to what we believe, we listen respectfully to one another, seek to discern all that is good and holy in each other's teachings, and cooperate in supporting everything that favors mutual understanding and peace.

5. The Jewish, Christian, and Muslim children and young people present here are a sign of hope and an incentive for us. Each new generation is a divine gift to the world. If we pass on to them all that is noble and good in our traditions, they will make it blossom in more intense brotherhood and cooperation.

If the various religious communities in the Holy City and in the Holy Land succeed in living and working together in friendship and harmony, this will be of enormous benefit not only to themselves but to the whole cause of peace in this region. Jerusalem will truly be a City of Peace for all peoples.

Then we will all repeat the words of the prophet: "Come, let us go up to the mountain of the Lord...that he may teach us his ways and that we may walk in his paths" (Isa 2:3). To recommit ourselves to such a task, and to do so in the Holy City of Jerusalem, is to ask God to look kindly on our efforts and bring them to a happy outcome. May the Almighty abundantly bless our common endeavors!

18. Homily at Outdoor Youth Mass at Korazim, Mount of the Beatitudes

March 24, 2000

1. "Consider your calling, brothers and sisters" (1 Cor 1:26).

Today these words of Saint Paul are addressed to all of us who have come here to the Mount of the Beatitudes. We sit on this hill like the first disciples, and we listen to Jesus. In the stillness, we hear his gentle and urgent voice, as gentle as this land itself and as urgent as a call to choose between life and death.

How many generations before us have been deeply moved by the Sermon on the Mount! How many young people down the centuries have gathered around Jesus to learn the words of eternal life, as you are gathered here today! How many young hearts have been inspired by the power of his personality and the compelling truth of his message! It is wonderful that you are here!...

This great gathering is like a rehearsal for the World Youth Day to be held in August in Rome! The young man who spoke promised that you will have another mountain, Mount Sinai. Young people of Israel, of the Palestinian Territories, of Jordan and Cyprus; young people of the Middle East, of Africa and Asia, of Europe, America, and Oceania! With love and affection I greet each one of you!

2. The first to hear the Beatitudes of Jesus bore in their hearts the memory of another mountain—Mount Sinai. Just a month ago, I had the grace of going there, where God spoke to Moses and gave the Law, "written with the finger of God" (Exod 31:18) on the tablets of stone. These two mountains—Sinai and the Mount of the Beatitudes—offer us the roadmap of our Christian life and a summary of our responsibilities to God and neighbor. The Law and the Beatitudes together mark the path of the following of Christ and the royal road to spiritual maturity and freedom.

The Ten Commandments of Sinai may seem negative: "You will have no false gods before me;...do not kill; do not commit adultery; do not steal; do not bear false witness." (Exod 20:3, 13–16). But in fact they are supremely positive. Moving beyond the evil they name, they point the way to the *law of love*, which is the first and greatest of the commandments: "You will love the Lord your God with all your heart, all your soul, and all your mind....You will love your neighbor as yourself" (Matt 22:37, 39). Jesus himself says that he came not to abolish but to fulfill the Law (see Matt 5:17). His message is new but it does not destroy what went before; it leads what went before to its fullest potential. Jesus teaches that the way of love brings the Law to fulfillment (see Gal 5:14). And he taught this enormously important truth on this hill here in Galilee.

3. "Blessed are you!" he says, "all you who are poor in spirit, gentle and merciful, you who mourn, who care for what is right, who are pure in heart, who make peace, you who are persecuted! Blessed are you!" But the words of Jesus may seem strange. It is strange that Jesus exalts those whom the world generally regards as weak. He says to them, "Blessed are you who seem to be losers, because you are the true winners: the kingdom of heaven is yours!" Spoken by him who is "gentle and humble in heart" (Matt 11:29), these words present a challenge which demands a deep and abiding *metanoia* of the spirit, a great change of heart.

You young people will understand why this change of heart is necessary! Because you are aware of another voice within you and all around you, a contradictory voice. It is a voice that says, "Blessed are the proud and violent, those who prosper at any cost, who are unscrupulous, pitiless, devious, who make war not peace, and persecute those who stand in their way." And this voice seems to make sense in a world where the violent often triumph and the devious seem to succeed. "Yes," says the voice of evil, "they are the ones who win. Happy are they!"

4. Jesus offers a very different message. Not far from this very place Jesus called his first disciples, as he calls you now. His call has always demanded a choice between the two voices competing for your hearts even now on this hill, the choice between good and evil, between life and death. Which voice will the young people of the twenty-first century choose to follow? To put your faith in Jesus means choosing to believe what he says, no matter how strange it may seem, and choosing to reject the claims of evil, no matter how sensible or attractive they may seem.

In the end, Jesus does not merely speak the Beatitudes. He lives the Beatitudes. He is the Beatitudes. Looking at him you will see what it means to be poor in spirit, gentle and merciful, to mourn, to care for what is right, to be pure in heart, to make peace, to be persecuted. This is why he has the right to say, "Come, follow *me!*" He does not say simply, "Do what I say." He says, "Come, follow *me!*"

You hear his voice on this hill, and you believe what he says. But like the first disciples at the Sea of Galilee, you must leave your boats and nets behind, and that is never easy—especially when you face an uncertain future and are tempted to lose faith in your Christian heritage. To be good Christians may seem beyond your strength in today's world. But Jesus does not stand by and leave you alone to face the challenge. He is always with you to transform your weakness into strength. Trust him when he says: "My grace is enough for you, for my power is made perfect in weakness" (2 Cor 12:9)!

5. The disciples spent time with the Lord. They came to know and love him deeply. They discovered the meaning of what the apostle Peter once said to Jesus: "Lord, to whom shall we go? You have the words of eternal life" (John 6:68). They discovered that the words of eternal life are the words of Sinai and the words of the Beatitudes. And this is the message that they spread everywhere.

At the moment of his ascension Jesus gave his disciples a mission and this reassurance: "All power in heaven and on earth has been given to me. Go, therefore, and make disciples of all nations...and behold I am with you always, until the end of the age" (Matt 28:18–20). For two thousand years Christ's followers have carried out this mission. Now, at the dawn of the third millennium, it is your turn. It is your turn to go out into the world to preach the message of the Ten Commandments and the Beatitudes. When God speaks, he speaks of things that have the greatest importance for each person, for the people of the twenty-first century no less than those of the first century. The Ten Commandments and the Beatitudes speak of truth and goodness, of grace and freedom: of all that is necessary to enter into Christ's Kingdom. Now it is your turn to be courageous apostles of that Kingdom!

Young people of the Holy Land, young people of the world: answer the Lord with a heart that is willing and open! Willing and open, like the heart of the greatest daughter of Galilee, Mary, the Mother of Jesus. How did she respond? She said: "I am the servant of the Lord; let it be done to me according to your word" (Luke 1:38).

O Lord Jesus Christ, in this place that you knew and loved so well, listen to these generous young hearts! Continue to teach these young people the truth of the Commandments and the Beatitudes! Make them joyful witnesses to your truth and convinced apostles of your Kingdom! Be with them always, especially when following you and the Gospel becomes difficult and demanding! You will be their strength; you will be their victory!

O Lord Jesus, you have made these young people your friends: keep them forever close to you! Amen.

19. Homily in the Basilica of the Annunciation, Nazareth

March 25, 2000

> "Behold the handmaid of the Lord.
> Be it done unto me according to your word."
> (Angelus Prayer)

Your Beatitude,
Brother Bishops,
Father *Custos,*
Dear Brothers and Sisters,

1. March 25th in the year 2000, the Solemnity of the Annunciation in the year of the Great Jubilee: on this day the eyes of the whole Church turn to Nazareth. I have longed to come back to the town of Jesus, to feel once

again, in contact with this place, the presence of the woman of whom Saint Augustine wrote: "He chose the mother he had created; he created the mother he had chosen" (*Sermo* 69, 3, 4). Here it is especially easy to understand why all generations call Mary blessed (Luke 1:48).

I warmly greet Your Beatitude Patriarch Michel Sabbah, and thank you for your kind words of presentation. With Archbishop Boutros Mouallem and all of you—bishops, priests, religious women and men, and members of the laity—I rejoice in the grace of this solemn celebration. I am happy to have this opportunity to greet the Franciscan Minister General, Father Giacomo Bini, who welcomed me on my arrival, and to express to the *Custos*, Father Giovanni Battistelli, and the Friars of the Custody the admiration of the whole Church for the devotion with which you carry out your unique vocation. With gratitude I pay tribute to your faithfulness to the charge given to you by Saint Francis himself and confirmed by the popes down the centuries.

2. We are gathered to celebrate the great mystery accomplished here two thousand years ago. The evangelist Luke situates the event clearly in time and place: "In the sixth month, the angel Gabriel was sent by God to a town in Galilee called Nazareth, to a virgin betrothed to a man named Joseph....The virgin's name was Mary" (1:26–27). But in order to understand what took place in Nazareth two thousand years ago, we must return to the reading from the Letter to the Hebrews. That text enables us, as it were, to listen to a conversation between the Father and the Son concerning God's purpose from all

eternity. "You who wanted no sacrifice or oblation pre-pared a body for me. You took no pleasure in holocausts or sacrifices for sin. Then I said,...'God, here I am! I am coming to obey your will'" (10:5–7). The Letter to the Hebrews is telling us that, in obedience to the Father's will, the Eternal Word comes among us to offer the sacri-fice that surpasses all the sacrifices offered under the for-mer covenant. His is the eternal and perfect sacrifice that redeems the world.

The divine plan is gradually revealed in the Old Testament, particularly in the words of the prophet Isaiah, which we have just heard: "The Lord himself will give you a sign. It is this: the virgin is with child and will soon give birth to a child whom she will call Emmanuel" (7:14). Emmanuel—God with us. In these words, the unique event that was to take place in Nazareth in the fullness of time is foretold, and it is this event that we are celebrating here with intense joy and happiness.

3. Our Jubilee Pilgrimage has been a journey in spirit, which began in the footsteps of Abraham, "our father in faith" (*Roman Canon;* cf. Rom 4:11–12). That journey has brought us today to Nazareth, where we meet Mary, the truest daughter of Abraham. It is Mary above all others who can teach us what it means to live the faith of "our father." In many ways, Mary is clearly different from Abraham; but in deeper ways "the friend of God" (Isa 41:8) and the young woman of Nazareth are very alike.

Both Abraham and Mary receive a wonderful promise from God. Abraham was to be the father of a son, from whom there would come a great nation. Mary is to be the

Mother of a Son who would be the Messiah, the Anointed One. "Listen!" Gabriel says, "You are to conceive and bear a son....The Lord God will give him the throne of his ancestor David...and his reign will have no end" (Luke 1:31–33).

For both Abraham and Mary, the divine promise comes as something completely unexpected. God disrupts the daily course of their lives, overturning its settled rhythms and conventional expectations. For both Abraham and Mary, the promise seems impossible. Abraham's wife Sarah was barren, and Mary is not yet married: "How can this come about," she asks, "since I am a virgin?" (Luke 1:34).

4. Like Abraham, Mary is asked to say yes to something that has never happened before. Sarah is the first in the line of barren wives in the Bible who conceive by God's power, just as Elizabeth will be the last. Gabriel speaks of Elizabeth to reassure Mary: "Know this too: your kinswoman Elizabeth has, in her old age, herself conceived a son" (Luke 1:36).

Like Abraham, Mary must walk through darkness, in which she must simply trust the One who called her. Yet even her question—"How can this come about?"—suggests that Mary is ready to say yes, despite her fears and uncertainties. Mary asks not whether the promise is possible, but only how it will be fulfilled. It comes as no surprise, therefore, when finally she utters her *fiat:* "I am the handmaid of the Lord. Let what you have said be done to me" (Luke 1:38). With these words, Mary shows herself the true daughter of Abraham, and she becomes the Mother of Christ and Mother of all believers.

5. In order to penetrate further into the mystery, let us look back to the moment of Abraham's journey when he received the promise. It was when he welcomed to his home three mysterious guests (Gen 18:1–15), and offered them the adoration due to God: *tres vidit et unum adoravit.* That mysterious encounter foreshadows the Annunciation, when Mary is powerfully drawn into communion with the Father, the Son, and the Holy Spirit. Through the *fiat* that Mary uttered in Nazareth, the Incarnation became the wondrous fulfillment of Abraham's encounter with God. So, following in the footsteps of Abraham, we have come to Nazareth to sing the praises of the woman "through whom the light rose over the earth" (Hymn *"Ave Regina Caelorum"*).

6. But we have also come to plead with her. What do we, pilgrims on our way into the third Christian millennium, ask of the Mother of God? Here in the town that Pope Paul VI, when he visited Nazareth, called "the school of the Gospel," where "we learn to look at and to listen to, to ponder and to penetrate the deep and mysterious meaning of the very simple, very humble, and very beautiful appearing of the Son of God" ("Address in Nazareth," January 5, 1964), I pray, first, for a great renewal of faith in all the children of the Church, a deep renewal of faith: not just as a general attitude of life, but as a conscious and courageous profession of the Creed: *"Et incarnatus est de Spiritu Sancto ex Maria Virgine, et homo factus est."*

In Nazareth, where Jesus "grew in wisdom and age and grace before God and men" (Luke 2:52), I ask the

Holy Family to inspire all Christians to defend the family against so many present-day threats to its nature, its stability, and its mission. To the Holy Family I entrust the efforts of Christians and of all people of good will to defend life and to promote respect for the dignity of every human being.

To Mary, the *Theotókos*, the great Mother of God, I consecrate the families of the Holy Land, the families of the world.

In Nazareth where Jesus began his public ministry, I ask Mary to help the Church everywhere to preach the "good news" to the poor, as he did (Luke 4:18). In this "year of the Lord's favor," I ask her to teach us the way of humble and joyful obedience to the Gospel in the service of our brothers and sisters, without preferences and without prejudices.

"O Mother of the Word Incarnate, despise not my petitions, but in your mercy hear and answer me. Amen" *(Memorare).*

20. Ecumenical Meeting with Greek Orthodox Patriarch of Jerusalem in the Old City of Jerusalem

March 25, 2000

Dear Brothers and Sisters in Christ,

1. With profound gratitude to the Most Holy Trinity I make this visit to the Greek Orthodox Patriarchate of Jerusalem, and I greet all of you in the grace and peace of

our Lord Jesus Christ. I thank Your Beatitude Patriarch Diodoros for your fraternal hospitality and for the kind words you have addressed to us. I greet Your Beatitude Patriarch Torkom, and all the archbishops and bishops of the Churches and ecclesial communities present. It is a source of great joy to know that the heads of Christian communities in the Holy City of Jerusalem meet frequently to deal with matters of common interest to the faithful. The fraternal spirit that prevails among you is a sign and a gift to the Christians of the Holy Land as they face the challenges before them.

Need I say that I am greatly encouraged by this evening's meeting? It confirms that we have set out on the path to knowing one another better, with the desire to overcome the mistrust and rivalry inherited from the past. Here in Jerusalem, in the city where our Lord Jesus Christ died and rose from the dead, his words ring out with special resonance, particularly the words he spoke on the night before he died: "that they may all be one;...so that the world may believe that you have sent me" (John 17:21). It is in response to that prayer of the Lord that we are together here, all followers of the one Lord despite our sad divisions, and all conscious that his will obliges us, and the Churches and ecclesial communities we represent, to walk the path of reconciliation and peace.

This meeting reminds me of the historic meeting here in Jerusalem between my predecessor Pope Paul VI and the Ecumenical Patriarch Athenagoras I, an event which laid the foundations of a new era of contacts between our Churches. In the intervening years we have learned that the road to unity is a difficult one. This should not discourage us. We must be patient and persevering, and continue to move ahead without wavering. The warm embrace of Pope Paul and Patriarch Athenagoras stands out as a prophetic sign and source of inspiration, urging us on to new efforts to respond to the Lord's will.

2. Our aspiration to fuller communion between Christians takes on a special meaning in the land of the Savior's birth and in the Holy City of Jerusalem. Here, in the presence of the different Churches and communities, I wish to reaffirm that the ecclesial note of universality fully respects legitimate diversity. The variety and beauty of your liturgical rites, and of your spiritual, theological, and canonical traditions and institutions, testifies to the richness of the divinely revealed and undivided heritage of the universal Church, as it has developed down the centuries in the East and in the West. There exists a legitimate diversity that in no way is opposed to the unity of the Body of Christ, but rather enhances the splendor of the Church and contributes greatly to the fulfillment of her mission (*Ut Unum Sint*, 50). None of this wealth must be lost in the fuller unity to which we aspire.

3. During the recent Week of Prayer for Christian Unity, in this year of the Great Jubilee, many of you joined in prayer for greater understanding and cooperation among all Christ's followers. You did so in the awareness that all the Lord's disciples together have a common mission to serve the Gospel in the Holy Land. The more united we become in prayer around Christ, the more courageous we shall become in confronting the painful human reality

of our divisions. The pilgrim path of the Church through this new century and the new millennium is the path traced out for her by her inherent vocation to unity. Let us ask the Lord to inspire a new spirit of harmony and solidarity among the Churches in facing the practical difficulties that beset the Christian community in Jerusalem and the Holy Land.

4. Fraternal cooperation among the Christians of this Holy City is no mere option; it has a significance all its own in communicating the love which the Father has for the world in sending his only Son (John 3:16). Only in a spirit of mutual respect and support can the Christian presence flourish here in a community alive with its traditions and confident in facing the social, cultural, and political challenges of an evolving situation. Only by being reconciled among themselves can Christians play their full part in making Jerusalem the City of Peace for all peoples. In the Holy Land, where Christians live side by side with the followers of Judaism and Islam, where there are almost daily tensions and conflicts, it is essential to overcome the scandalous impression given by our disagreements and arguments. In this city it should be eminently possible for Christians, Jews, and Muslims to live together in brotherhood and freedom, in dignity, justice, and peace.

5. Dear Brothers in Christ, it has been my intention to give a clearly ecumenical dimension to the Catholic Church's celebration of the Jubilee Year 2000. The opening of the Holy Door at the Basilica of Saint Paul Outside the Walls, at which so many Churches and ecclesial com-

munities were represented, symbolized our passing together through the "door" that is Christ: "I am the door, if anyone enters by me, he will be saved" (John 10:9). Our ecumenical journey is precisely this: a journey in Christ and through Christ the Savior to the faithful fulfillment of the Father's plan. With God's grace the two-thousandth anniversary of the Incarnation of the Word will be a "favorable time," a year of grace for the ecumenical movement. In the spirit of the Old Testament Jubilees, this is a providential time for us to turn to the Lord in order to ask forgiveness for the wounds which the members of our Churches have inflicted upon one another down the years. This is the time to ask the Spirit of Truth to help our Churches and communities to engage in an ever more fruitful theological dialogue, which will enable us to grow in the knowledge of the truth and come to the fullness of communion in Christ's Body. From the exchange of ideas our dialogue will then become an exchange of gifts: a more authentic sharing of the love that the Spirit unceasingly pours into our hearts.

Your Beatitude reminded us of Christ's prayer on the eve of his passion and death. This prayer is his last will and testament, and it challenges us all. What will be our response? Dear Brothers in Christ, with hope-filled hearts and unfailing trust, let us make the third Christian millennium the millennium of our new-found joy in the unity and peace of the Father, the Son, and the Holy Spirit. Amen.

21. Prayer for Forgiveness Placed in the Wailing Wall, Jerusalem

March 26, 2000

God of our fathers,
you chose Abraham and his descendants
to bring your Name to the Nations:
we are deeply saddened by the behavior of those
who in the course of history
have caused these children of yours to suffer,
and asking your forgiveness we wish to commit
    ourselves
to genuine brotherhood
with the people of the Covenant.
We ask this through Christ our Lord. Amen.

22. Homily in the Church of the Holy Sepulcher, Jerusalem

March 26, 2000

"I believe in Jesus Christ...conceived by the power of the Holy Spirit and born of the Virgin Mary. He suffered under Pontius Pilate, was crucified, died, and was buried....On the third day he rose again."

1. Following the path of salvation history, as narrated in the Apostles' Creed, my Jubilee Pilgrimage has brought me to the Holy Land. From Nazareth, where Jesus was conceived of the Virgin Mary by the power of the Holy Spirit, I have reached Jerusalem, where he "suffered

under Pontius Pilate, was crucified, died, and was buried." Here, in the Church of the Holy Sepulcher, I kneel before the place of his burial: "Behold, the place where they laid him" (Mark 16:6).

The tomb is empty. It is a silent witness to the central event of human history: the resurrection of our Lord Jesus Christ. For almost two thousand years the empty tomb has borne witness to the victory of life over death. With the apostles and evangelists, with the Church of every time and place, we too bear witness and proclaim: "Christ is risen! Raised from the dead he will never die again; death no longer has power over him" (Rom 6:9).

"Mors et vita duello conflixere mirando; dux vitae mortuus, regnat vivus" (Latin Easter Sequence, *Victimae Paschali*). The Lord of Life was dead; now he reigns, victorious over death, the source of everlasting life for all who believe.

2. In this, "the Mother of all Churches" (St. John Damascene), I extend warm greetings to His Beatitude Patriarch Michel Sabbah, the Ordinaries of the other Catholic communities, Father Giovanni Battistelli and the Franciscan Friars of the Custody of the Holy Land, as well as the clergy, religious, and lay faithful.

With fraternal esteem and affection I greet Patriarch Diodoros of the Greek Orthodox Church and Patriarch Torkom of the Armenian Orthodox Church, the representatives of the Coptic, Syrian, and Ethiopian Churches, as well as of the Anglican and Lutheran Communities.

Here, where our Lord Jesus Christ died in order to gather into one the children of God who were scattered

(John 11:52), may the Father of mercies strengthen our desire for unity and peace among all who have received the gift of new life through the saving waters of Baptism.

3. "Destroy this temple and in three days I will raise it up" (John 2:19).

The evangelist John tells us that, after Jesus rose from the dead, the disciples remembered these words, and they believed (John 2:22). Jesus had spoken these words that they might be a sign for his disciples. When he and the disciples visited the Temple, he expelled the money-changers and vendors from the holy place (John 2:15). When those present protested, saying: "What sign have you to show us for doing this?" Jesus replied: "Destroy this temple and in three days I will raise it up." The evangelist observes that he "was speaking of the temple of his body" (John 2:18–21).

The prophecy contained in Jesus' words was fulfilled at Easter, when "on the third day he rose from the dead." The resurrection of our Lord Jesus Christ is the sign that the Eternal Father is faithful to his promise and brings new life out of death: "the resurrection of the body and life everlasting." The mystery is clearly reflected in this ancient Church of the *Anástasis*, which contains both the empty tomb—the sign of the resurrection—and Golgotha—the place of the crucifixion. The Good News of the resurrection can never be separated from the mystery of the cross. Saint Paul tells us this in today's second reading: "We preach Christ crucified" (1 Cor 1:23). Christ, who offered himself as an evening sacrifice on the altar of the cross (Ps 141:2), has now been revealed as "the power of God and the wisdom of God" (1 Cor 1:24). And in his resurrection, the sons and daughters of Adam have been made sharers in the divine life that was his from all eternity, with the Father, in the Holy Spirit.

4. "I am the Lord your God, who brought you out of the land of Egypt, out of the house of bondage" (Exod 20:2).

Today's Lenten liturgy sets before us the covenant that God made with his people on Mount Sinai, when he gave the Ten Commandments of the Law to Moses. Sinai represents the second stage of that great pilgrimage of faith that began when God said to Abraham: "Go from your country and your kindred and your father's house to the land that I will show you" (Gen 12:1).

The Law and the covenant are the seal of the promise made to Abraham. Through the Decalogue and the moral law inscribed on the human heart (Rom 2:15), God radically challenges the freedom of every man and woman. To respond to God's voice resounding in the depths of our conscience and to choose good is the most sublime use of human freedom. It is, in a real sense, to make the choice between life and death (see Deut 30:15). By walking the path of the covenant with the All-Holy God, the people became bearers and witnesses of the promise, the promise of genuine liberation and fullness of life.

The resurrection of Jesus is the definitive seal of all God's promises, the birthplace of a new, risen humanity, the pledge of a history marked by the Messianic gifts of peace and spiritual joy. At the dawn of a new millennium, Christians can and ought to look to the future with steadfast trust in the glorious power of the Risen One to make all things new (Rev 21:5). He is the One who frees all creation from its bondage to futility (Rom 8:20). By his resurrection he opens the way to the great Sabbath rest, the Eighth Day, when mankind's pilgrimage will come to its end and God will be all in all (1 Cor 15:28).

Here at the Holy Sepulcher and Golgotha, as we renew our profession of faith in the Risen Lord, can we doubt that in the power of the Spirit of Life we will be given the strength to overcome our divisions and to work together to build a future of reconciliation, unity, and peace? Here, as in no other place on earth, we hear the Lord say once again to his disciples: "Do not fear; I have overcome the world!" (John 16:33).

5. *"Mors et vita duello conflixere mirando; dux vitae mortuus, regnat vivus."*

Radiant with the glory of the Spirit, the Risen Lord is the Head of the Church, his Mystical Body. He sustains her in her mission of proclaiming the Gospel of salvation to the men and women of every generation, until he returns in glory!

From this place, where the resurrection was first made known to the women and then to the apostles, I urge all the Church's members to renew their obedience to the Lord's command to take the Gospel to all the ends of the earth. At the dawn of a new millennium, there is a great need to proclaim from the rooftops the Good News that "God so loved the world that he gave his only Son, that whoever believes in him should not perish, but have eternal life" (John 3:16).

"Lord, you have the words of eternal life" (John 6:68). Today, as the unworthy successor of Peter, I wish to repeat these words as we celebrate the Eucharistic Sacrifice in this, the most hallowed place on earth. With all of redeemed humanity, I make my own the words that Peter the Fisherman spoke to the Christ, the Son of the living God: "Lord, to whom shall we go? You have the words of eternal life."

Christós anésti.

Jesus Christ is risen! He is truly risen! Amen.

The Pope's "Ascent to Calvary"

After morning Mass in the Church of the Holy Sepulcher, the pope wished to pray in the Chapel of Calvary, but was told that his tight schedule for the rest of the day prevented that. Father Luis Terrato, Superior of Basilica of the Holy Sepulcher, said that the pope's disappointment was obvious and that he "left the Holy Sepulcher with a thorn in his heart."

Even so, Fr. Terrato was surprised when, about four in the afternoon, just after vespers, the pope returned. There was some concern about the narrow twenty-two step staircase leading up to the chapel, but John Paul II "went up the steep little stairway leading to the chapel with effort but with great energy," Fr. Tarrato said. "It was like an ascent to Calvary and he suffered doing it, but he did it: he went to the place of the 'Pieta' of Calvary and he prayed there a good while. We left him alone because he had come there to pray."

Fr. Terrato continued: "During the homily, [the pope] spoke about the Resurrection and Calvary: given that there is a profound unity between the death and resurrection of Christ, it seemed that without an ascent to Calvary there was something lacking from his trip. This is why, I think, he wanted to complete his pilgrimage this way."

23. Angelus Message, Jerusalem

March 26, 2000

Dear Brothers and Sisters,

These have been days of intense emotion, a time when our soul has been stirred not only by the memory of what God has done but by his very presence, walking with us once again in the land of Christ's birth, death, and resurrection. And at every step of this Jubilee Pilgrimage Mary has been with us, lighting our pilgrim path and sharing the joys and sorrows of her sons and daughters.

With Mary, *Mater dolorosa*, we stand in the shadow of the cross and weep with her over the affliction of Jerusalem and over the sins of the world. We stand with her in the silence of Calvary, and see the blood and water flowing from the wounded side of her Son. Realizing the terrible consequences of sin, we are moved to repentance for our own sins and for the sins of the Church's children in every age. O Mary, conceived without sin, help us on the path to conversion!

With Mary, *Stella matutina,* we have been touched by the light of the resurrection. We rejoice with her that the empty tomb has become the womb of eternal life, where he who rose from the dead now sits at the Father's right hand. With her we give endless thanks for the grace of the Holy Spirit whom the Risen Lord sent upon the Church at Pentecost and whom he continually pours into our hearts, for our salvation and for the good of the human family.

Mary, *Regina in caelum assumpta.* From the tomb of her Son, we look to the tomb where Mary lay sleeping in peace, awaiting her glorious assumption. The Divine Liturgy celebrated at her tomb in Jerusalem has Mary say: "Even beyond death, I am not far from you." And in the liturgy her children reply: "Seeing your tomb, O holy Mother of God, we seem to contemplate you. O Mary, you are the joy of the angels, the comfort of the afflicted. We proclaim you as the stronghold of all Christians and, most of all, as Mother." In contemplating the *Theotókos,* almost at this journey's end, we look upon the true face of the Church, radiant in all her beauty, shining with "the glory of God which is on the face of Christ" (2 Cor 4:6). O Advocate, help the Church to be ever more like you, her exalted model. Help her to grow in faith, hope, and love, as she searches out and does the will of God in all things (*Lumen Gentium,* 65). O clement, O loving, O sweet Virgin Mary!

Pope John Paul II's
Holy Land Pilgrimage:
A Jewish Appraisal

Yehezkel Landau

*H*e came to the Holy Land as a pilgrim, a man of prayer, to bring a message of peace. Earlier in the Jubilee Year 2000, he had identified with Abraham's journey from Ur of the Chaldeans to the land then called Canaan. Afterwards he traveled to Mount Sinai to identify with Moses' journey through the wilderness with the Israelites. At the spot where the Torah was revealed, he affirmed the Ten Commandments as essential for reconsecrating private and public morality in our time. And then, on the first leg of his Holy Land pilgrimage, he stood atop Mount Nebo to view the Promised Land from Moses' final resting place.

As he flew into Ben Gurion Airport on March 21, 2000, John Paul II was making his 91st international trip as pope. For many, this was *the* journey, par excellence, of his long and remarkable pontificate. For Jews, especially Israeli Jews, the papal visit was a watershed in the history of our relations with Christianity, and with Catholicism in particular. For all of humanity, it was, I believe, a metahistorical event in which the combination of person, place, and time produced a *kairos* moment transcending political divisions and offering a glimpse of true holiness. For Jews and Muslims locked in mortal combat over Israel/Palestine, the humble witness of this frail pilgrim pope demonstrated the potential of Christians to be peacemakers, which is to be, in the spirit of the Beatitudes, true "children of God." In his words and deeds along his route, this pope sought, on behalf of Christians everywhere, to make amends for two millennia of persecution toward both Jews and Muslims, the elder and younger siblings in the Abrahamic family of faith.

For Christian-Jewish relations, the pontiff's Holy Land pilgrimage broke new ground, both theologically and politically. To fully understand its impact on both levels, some historical context is needed. But first I offer a vignette from my own life journey. The context for this episode, my only direct encounter with the pope, is my peacebuilding work in the Holy Land over the past twenty-six years. In 1991, shortly after the Gulf War—when I was a reserve soldier serving with my Israeli army unit at Sha'arei Tzedek Hospital in Jerusalem, simulating with the medical staff the intake of hundreds of chemical warfare victims—I attended an interfaith conference in Italy convened by the World Conference on Religion and Peace. The gathering focused on peacebuilding in the Middle East. On July 4, the conference participants were bused from Castel Gandolfo, outside Rome, to the Vatican for an audience with John Paul II. In his prepared remarks before our group, the pontiff expressed his support for our religiously motivated peacemaking efforts.

After his speech, the pope greeted each member of our group. When I was introduced to him by name, with the geographic coordinate "from Jerusalem," I shook his hand and said to him, "Shalom! I hope you grace us with your presence soon." He simply nodded and said nothing in response. Almost nine years later, I was privileged to be in Jerusalem as the pope traversed the land, as Abraham had done, spreading his message of justice, love, and reconciliation and touching the hearts of all who watched and listened in amazement. I recall standing on a rooftop in East Jerusalem, watching the pope's motorcade wind its way through the streets of the city and eventually pass the spot where I stood in order to get to the apostolic delegate's home on the Mount of Olives, where the pontiff was staying. Later in the week I was in the audience at an interfaith event at the Notre Dame Center. This was the one event during the papal visit that deteriorated into political rancor and disarray. (More on that unfortunate incident below.) Given the risks and potential land mines that beset the pope's journey, the fact that only one event turned sour underscored the generally positive, indeed inspirational, nature of his extraordinary pilgrimage.

In the Middle East, memory is both a blessing and a curse. For the Arab Muslims, the Crusades happened yesterday. Israeli Jews, not only Holocaust survivors, can not forget two millennia of disdain, hatred, and murderous assaults by ostensibly faithful Christians, including popes. For any Jew, a visit to Rome evokes haunting memories:

the Jewish ghetto and the Arch of Titus depicting the menorah from the Second Temple carried away as a spoil of war. For centuries, newly elected popes would stop at the Arch of Titus on their way to St. Peter's Basilica for their coronation. At that spot, symbolizing the defeat and humiliation of the Jewish people, the new pope would receive a Torah scroll from a Jewish representative. He would then hand it back, saying, "I receive this book from you, but not your interpretation of it." This custom reflected the supersessionist theology and the "teaching of contempt" that characterized Catholicism until the Second Vatican Council.

During the pontificate of John Paul II, so much has happened to transform that tragic history of persecution and suffering. Indeed, it is safe to say that this pope has done more than anyone else in history to advance the cause of Christian-Jewish reconciliation. His historic visits to the Rome synagogue and the Auschwitz death camp were but two of the landmark events of his tenure as pontiff. The establishment of formal diplomatic relations between the Holy See and the State of Israel, a revolutionary development awaited by Jews for years, would not have come about without the pope's blessing and encouragement. In his meetings with Jewish leaders, in Rome and elsewhere, he reiterated his condemnation of anti-Semitism and his fraternal solidarity with Jews as "elder brothers." And Jews knew that his words carried the authenticity of his life experience. His childhood friendships with Jews in Wadowice, Poland, helped him to later identify with the indescribable suffering of the Jewish people during the *Shoah* and with their yearning for freedom, dignity, and national renewal in a sovereign Jewish state.

By the time John Paul II came to Israel in March of 2000, much of the foundation for Catholic-Jewish rapprochement had already been laid. And yet Jews, especially in Israel, were still suspicious, wondering what his motives for visiting were. Partly this was because few Jews are aware of the spiritual and theological sea change that many church leaders have undergone in their relationships toward Jews and Judaism in the last half-century. This widespread ignorance made the pope's symbolic pilgrimage all the more astounding to most Jews. To appreciate just how remarkable the papal visit was for Israelis, consider this: In arithmetic classes, Israeli Jewish schoolchildren are taught to make a small inverted T rather than a cross when adding numbers. (One of Christianity's most sacred symbols evokes aversion in many Jews, given the long history of pogroms on Good Friday and following the enactment of passion plays). Despite this common practice in Israeli schools, when the pope's Jubilee journey was covered on Israeli television, the Hebrew words for *pilgrimage (aliyah leregel)* included a small cross instead of the letter *yod*.

Most observers would agree that the historic turning point in Catholic-Jewish relations was the *Nostra Aetate* statement issued on October 28, 1965, by the Second Vatican Council. The council, convened originally by the beloved Pope John XXIII, extended over four years after its inaugural session on October 11, 1962. The document referring to the Jewish people was one of sixteen conciliar texts, and it bears the official title: "Declaration on the Relation of the Church to Non-Christian Religions." After centuries of triumphalism, praying for the conversion of the "perfidious Jews" on Good Friday, the Roman Catholic Church changed its official stance. It still affirmed that it is "in duty bound to proclaim without fail Christ who is the way, the truth, and the life" (John 1:6), that in Christ "God reconciled all things to himself [and so] people find the fullness of their religious life" in Christianity, and that the church "believes that Christ who is our peace has through his cross reconciled Jews and Gentiles and made them one in himself." Yet, together with this classical formulation of Christian faith, the council was able to detoxify the most poisonous element in Jewish-Christian relations over the centuries: the accusation that the Jews were guilty of crucifying Christ and were rejected and punished by God for this cosmic crime of deicide. *Nostra Aetate* (the first two words in the Latin version) repudiated this heinous libel once and for all. While it does refer generally to "other religions" in a positive light and states that "the Church looks with esteem" upon Muslims in particular, the declaration is best remembered for its revolutionary statements about the Jews:[1]

> As holy Scripture testifies, Jerusalem did not recognize the time of her visitation (cf. Luke 19:44), nor did Jews in large number accept the Gospel; indeed, not a few

---

1. From *The Documents of Vatican II*, ed. Walter M. Abbott, SJ (New York: The America Press, 1966), 660–68.

opposed the spreading of it (cf. Rom 11:28). Nevertheless, according to the Apostle, the Jews still remain most dear to God because of their fathers, for He does not repent of the gifts He makes nor of the calls He issues (cf. Rom 11:28–29)....

True, authorities of the Jews and those who followed their lead pressed for the death of Christ (cf. John 19:6); still, what happened in His passion cannot be blamed upon all the Jews then living, without distinction, nor upon the Jews of today. Although the Church is the new people of God, the Jews should not be presented as repudiated or cursed by God, as if such views followed from the holy Scriptures. All should take pains, then, lest in catechetical instruction and in the preaching of God's Word they teach anything out of harmony with the truth of the gospel and the spirit of Christ.

The Church repudiates all persecutions against any man. Moreover, mindful of her common patrimony with the Jews, and *motivated by the gospel's spiritual love and by no political considerations*, she deplores the hatred, persecutions, and displays of anti-Semitism directed against the Jews at any time and from any source [emphasis added].[2]

These statements merit some analysis, especially in light of subsequent events. (The recent controversy over Mel Gibson's film *The Passion of the Christ*, for example, serves to underscore how sensitive these issues are, and how Jewish-Christian relations are still adversely affected by the demonization of Jews by Christians over many cen-

---

2. Ibid., p. 667.

turies.) Why the explicit denial of any "political consider-ations" as a factor in condemning anti-Semitism? Why, instead, the affirmation of a single justification for this theological transformation: "the gospel's spiritual love"? To understand this argument, we need to examine the speech delivered to the participants in Vatican II by Cardinal Augustin Bea, SJ. Cardinal Bea, then president of the Secretariat for Promoting Christian Unity, was the person most responsible for getting the *Nostra Aetate* text adopted. He was commissioned personally for this assign-ment by Pope John XXIII. In order to overcome opposition to the document as it was being considered, Bea delivered a speech in defense of the new theological stance being promulgated. Here are excerpts from his remarks, part of the "oral tradition" accompanying the *Nostra Aetate* text:[3]

> The decree [on the Jews] is very brief, but the material treated in it is not easy. Let us enter immediately into the heart of it and tell what we are talking about. Or rather, since it is so easy to understand it wrongly, before all else let us say what we are not talking about. There is no national or political question here. Especially is there no question of acknowledging the State of Israel on the part of the Holy See...There is only treatment of a purely religious question....
>
> There are those who object: Did not the princes of this people, with the people in agreement, condemn and crucify the innocent Christ, the Lord? Did they not

---

3. "Catholics and Jews," in *Council Speeches of Vatican II*, eds. Hans Küng, Yves Congar, OP, and Daniel O'Hanlon, SJ (New York/Glen Rock, NJ: Paulist Press, 1964), 254–61; here, edited from 254–58.

"clamor": "Let his blood be upon us and upon our children" (Matt. 27:25)? Did not Christ himself speak most severely about Jews and their punishment?

I reply simply and briefly: It is true that Christ spoke severely, but only with the intention that the people might be converted and might "recognize the time of its visitation" (Luke 19:42–49). But even as he is dying on the cross he prays: "Father forgive them, for they know not what they do" (Luke 23:34).

Wherefore, since the Lord emphasized, before the burial of Lazarus, speaking to the Father: "I know that thou always hearest me" (John 11:42), it is wrong to say that his prayer to the Father was not heard and that God has not only not forgiven the fault of his chosen people but that he has rejected them....

The point, therefore, is not in any way to call into doubt—as is sometimes falsely asserted—the events which are narrated in the Gospels about Christ's consciousness of his dignity and divine nature, or about the manner in which the innocent Lord was unjustly condemned. Rather that, with these things kept fully in mind, it is still possible and necessary to imitate the gentle charity of Christ the Lord and his Apostles with which they excused their persecutors.

Bea then asked his colleagues: "But *why is it so necessary precisely today* to recall these things?" (italics in the original text). He answered that the "propaganda" against the Jews that was spread by the Nazis needed to be rooted out from the minds of Catholics and replaced by the truth of Christianity. He condemned National Socialism's "particularly violent and criminal form" of anti-Semitism, "which through hatred for the Jews committed frightful crimes, extirpating several millions of Jewish people..." And he argued for the application of Christian love and forgiveness: "If Christ the Lord and the Apostles who personally experienced the sorrows of the crucifixion embraced their very persecutors with an ardent charity, how much more must we be motivated by the same charity?"[4] We see here how Bea's thinking informed the text of *Nostra Aetate.*

In his speech, Bea declared that "the Jews of our times can hardly be accused of the crimes committed against Christ, so far removed are they from those deeds. Actually, even in the time of Christ, the majority of the chosen people did not cooperate with the leaders of the people in condemning Christ."[5] Bea combined two arguments: the Jews as a whole, then and now, are not culpable for the crucifixion, and those who *were* guilty, at that time, have been forgiven by God, both the Father and the Son. Consequently, he concludes his remarks by stressing that, for the council, what should be "simply decisive" is "the example of burning charity of the Lord himself on the cross praying 'Father, forgive them, for they know not what they are doing.' This is the example to be imitated by the Church, the bride of Christ. This is the road to be followed by her. This is what the schema proposed by us intends to foster and promote."[6]

From Bea's speech, we get a clearer idea of the theological rationale behind *Nostra Aetate's* declaration excul-

---

4. Ibid., 258–59.
5. Ibid., 259.
6. Ibid., 261.

pating the Jews from the deicide accusation. And what of the "political considerations" that might otherwise be imputed to the drafters of this historic conciliar document? We saw above that Bea disavowed any recognition of the State of Israel by the Holy See. (That watershed in 1993 was due largely to John Paul II's leadership.) Toward the end of his speech, Bea returned to this thorny subject of statehood and said: "Lastly: since we are here treating a merely religious question, there is obviously no danger that the Council will get entangled in those difficult questions regarding the relations between the Arab nations and the State of Israel, or regarding so-called Zionism."[7]

For most Jews, Judaism and Zionism are so intertwined in their self-understanding that it is impossible to separate the two. The tendency of many Christians, including Catholics, to make that distinction (based on their own tradition of separating God and Caesar), has caused much misunderstanding and ill will in Jewish-Christian relations in recent decades—at least until the Holy See recognized the State of Israel. The political and theological considerations are interrelated, and always were, despite Bea's rhetorical dichotomy.

To fully appreciate the importance of Pope John Paul II's Jubilee pilgrimage to Israel/Palestine in 2000, we need, first of all, to recall the two millennia of Christian persecution of Jews and contempt for Judaism. In this light, Cardinal Bea's plea to his colleagues to forgive the Jews as Christ and the Apostles did—for a crime they did

---

7. Ibid.

not even commit (since it was the Romans who crucified Jesus)—sounds absurd and outrageous to Jewish ears. But this is as far as the Church was ready to go in 1965.

The years following were characterized by further movement away from the notion that the Jews needed to be forgiven, as a gesture of "Christian charity," for anything they might have done. One can cite, as one of many benchmarks, the 1985 speech delivered by Cardinal Johannes Willebrands, who worked under Cardinal Bea at Vatican II and then succeeded him as head of the Secretariat for Promoting Christian Unity. Cardinal Willebrands's presentation at Westminster Cathedral in London was, in fact, the Cardinal Bea Memorial Lecture for that year. In his speech,[8] Willebrands reviewed the progress made in Christian-Jewish relations in the twenty years since *Nostra Aetate*. He noted that "a certain amount of trust has been generated" on the Jewish side, and that "some, if not all, barriers have been torn down." Regarding the Christian side, he said that "we in the Church have become, or are becoming, aware of our historical and our theological responsibilities toward our elder brother, grounded in the link the Council spoke about."

The cardinal stressed the common challenge of combating famine, oppression, and the plight of refugees worldwide. He said that "Jews and Christians, right across the board, are called in the name of their common bibli-

8. "Christians and Jews: A New Vision," in *Vatican II Revisited by Those Who Were There*, ed. Alberic Stacpoole (Minneapolis: Winston Press, 1986), 220–36.

cal heritage to stand up and do something together..." He understood that such joint action would bring to the surface some underlying tensions in the Christian-Jewish relationship:

> I am not blind to the issues such a decision will raise, or has already raised. The main issue also becomes, once the twenty years of first encounters have elapsed, one of the main challenges we have to face—perhaps the greatest. It thus becomes also a significant part of our task for the future. I refer to the asymmetry between our Catholic and Jewish communities or, better still, between Church and Judaism. The Church is a Church, a worldwide religious community orientated mainly to the glory of God and the ministry of salvation of those called to her bosom. It has, as such, no particular ethnic or cultural identity; every man and woman from any background should feel at home with her. Judaism is a very different matter. While defined by some as an instrument of redemption, it is at the same time, and almost in the same breath, a people with a definite ethnicity, a culture, with an intrinsic reference to a land and a State. These differences should by now be obvious, but it is an open question whether we are on each side well enough aware of all the implications thereof. It means, at the very least, that agendas do not always coincide, priorities are not necessarily the same and concerns can go very different ways.[9]

These are sound observations. They were confirmed later when Jews and Catholics found themselves on differ-

9. Ibid., p. 233.

ent sides of painful controversies, such as the one that arose over the Carmelite convent at Auschwitz or the mutual misunderstandings around the elevation to saint-hood of the Jewish Carmelite nun Edith Stein/Teresa Benedicta. At another point in Willebrands's speech, he asserted:

> Jewish-Christian relations are an unending affair, as are love and brotherhood, but also (regrettably) hatred and enmity. The main point is to change the funda-mental orientation, from hatred to love, from enmity to brotherhood. It is not a question only of deploying doc-uments, or of particular actions, however highly placed those who act happen to be. It is a question of people, men and women of flesh and blood. Still more, it is a question of hearts.[10]

This statement surely pertains to the pope's Jubilee pilgrimage to the Holy Land: it was obviously a media event with the pope as the central celebrity, and as such it was a public witness on a global stage. But it was, above all, a witness that touched and moved hearts, millions if not billions of human hearts. Love and brotherhood were not just proclaimed; they were embodied in a man of flesh and blood whose flesh was old and weak, but whose spirit was strong and vibrant and radiated compassion for all.

At the Yad Vashem Holocaust Memorial Museum, this frail and elderly pontiff stood next to a youthful and vig-orous Israeli prime minister, Ehud Barak, a military com-mando and commander turned statesman. What a role

---

10. Ibid., pp. 229–30.

reversal that iconographic image was, in contrast to the familiar juxtaposition of two female characters representing a feeble, blindfolded Synagogue alongside the Church triumphant. But that visual anomaly at Yad Vashem, which was not lost on Israeli Jews,[11] was reinforced by the genuineness of the pope's solidarity with Jewish suffering. That heartfelt solidarity was evidenced in his words and even more by the affection he displayed toward his survivor friends from Wadowice, who were present for this ceremonial event. One of them was Edith Tzirer, who was liberated from a concentration camp in January 1945, almost paralyzed by tuberculosis and other afflictions. Karol Wojtyla, the present pope, was then a seminarian when he met young Edith and gave her food and drink. He then carried her for almost two miles, from the camp to the local railroad station. After regaining her health, Edith later moved to Israel. Aside from this very moving personal dimension, the event at Yad Vashem was laden with deep symbolic meaning, both political and religious—and these two dimensions could not be separated. The two men were the recognized leaders of two communities of faith represented by two sovereign entities, the State of Israel and the Holy See. The agreement establishing diplomatic relations between them, fostered by John Paul II, had put their relations on an unprecedented footing. Ehud Barak, whose grandparents perished at Dachau, represented a Jewish people that had survived

---

11. See Yossi Klein Halevi, "Zionism's Gift," *The New Republic*, April 10, 2000, p. 6.

genocide, had established its own flourishing state, and was now able to host the Bishop of Rome from a position of strength and pride. It was the ceremony at Yad Vashem, more than any other event during the papal pilgrimage, that symbolized this new, healthier relationship between Jews and Catholics. And it was that historic transformation of power relations, identities, and shared memories that allowed Prime Minister Barak to declare that the Jewish people has a friend in the Vatican.

Despite appeals from other Jews, Barak did not berate his guest for failing to issue an outright apology for the Church's actions during the *Shoah,* including the reticence of Pope Pius XII. Nor did Barak lament the limited access granted to the Vatican archives from that period. Barak understood that magnanimity and fraternal solidarity were the qualities to exhibit on that extraordinary occasion. He praised the Righteous Gentiles who had risked their lives to save Jews, and among them he counted John Paul II. "You have done more than anyone to apply the Church's historic change toward the Jewish people, a change begun by the good Pope John XXIII." Barak called the pope's visit to Yad Vashem "the climax of this historic journey of healing."

The spiritual message of the moment was deepened by John Paul II's expression of deep sadness for the suffering Jews have experienced at the hands of Christians throughout history. In his address he acknowledged that silence spoke more powerfully than words in the face of such horrors and traumatic memories. And those memories, he declared, serve a purpose looking toward the future: "to ensure that never again will evil prevail, as it did for the millions of innocent victims of Nazism....Jews and Christians share an immense spiritual patrimony, flowing from God's self-revelation. Our religious teachings and our spiritual experience demand that we overcome evil with good" (full speech here on pp. 98-101). The psalmist, in describing the person who savors life, exhorts: "Depart from evil and do good; seek peace, and pursue it" (Ps. 34:15). The good that John Paul II did on his Holy Land trip, with his fervent appeals for peace and justice, served to combat the evils of prejudice, hatred, and war.

The culmination of his six-day sojourn among us, at least in the eyes of Jews, came with his visit to the Western Wall, in Hebrew the *Kotel Ha-Ma'aravi.* Rabbi Michael Melchior, representing the Israeli Government as Minister for Diaspora Affairs, welcomed the pope to that sacred site and presented to him an ornate Bible as a personal gift. When the pontiff shuffled slowly toward those immense stones, placed his prayer of contrition inside a crack in the wall, and remained there to offer his solitary confession before God at the spot that is most holy to our people, Jews everywhere were stunned by this simple yet profound gesture. Ironically, the prayer that he left in the *Kotel* was the same one uttered just days before as part of a litany of penitential confession in St. Peter's Basilica:

God of our fathers,
You chose Abraham and his descendants
to bring your Name to the Nations;

we are deeply saddened
by the behaviour of those
who in the course of history
have caused these children of yours to suffer
and asking your forgiveness
we wish to commit ourselves
to genuine brotherhood
with the people of the Covenant.

Some Jews had complained, when this prayer was read out at St. Peter's, that it was not explicit enough in specifying the crimes committed by Christians against Jews or in offering an explicit apology. But the same words took on their true resonance and power when they were brought from Rome to Jerusalem, to be placed by the pope in the Wall which abuts the Temple Mount and the Holy of Holies. This was another iconographic moment, coming near the end of John Paul II's pilgrimage, when person, place, and time converged in historic terms. Instead of gloating triumphantly over the loss of the ancient Temple at the hands of the Romans, instead of rubbing salt in the collective Jewish wound symbolized by the Arch of Titus, this pontiff came from Rome to the Western Wall to ask God's forgiveness for the two millennia of harm that Christians have caused Jews. And through this act of sincere repentance, the pope embodied, in the most direct and powerful way possible, the new era of transformed relations between Christians and Jews. Instead of asking his fellow Catholics to forgive Jews for killing Christ, as Cardinal Bea and *Nostra Aetate* had done, John Paul II acknowledged that it is Christians who are in need of forgiveness for what they have perpetrated against Jews. Jews, in turn, should acknowledge with gratitude this *metanoia* (in Hebrew, *teshuvah:* moral transformation or repentance) on the part of the Church. Only then can we Jews join our Catholic partners in building a more blessed future for everyone, in the spirit of Cardinal Willebrands's remarks in 1985.

Against the backdrop of this appreciative assessment of the pope's pilgrimage, some words should be said about the Jewish-Christian-Muslim trialogue at the Notre Dame Center that turned into a fiasco. The pope was joined for this symbolic occasion by Israeli Ashkenazi Chief Rabbi Lau and Sheikh Tamimi representing the Palestinian Authority.

Rabbi Lau spoke first, delivering a positive message advocating peaceful relations among the religions. But he concluded with a statement of gratitude to the pope for recognizing that Jerusalem is the "eternal, undivided capital" of Israel and the Jewish people. By attributing this political stance to John Paul II, the rabbi sparked a vehement reaction from the Palestinians present. From my seat in the balcony, I could hear my Palestinian Catholic friend Afif Safieh, ambassador to the United Kingdom and the Holy See on behalf of the Palestinian Authority, shouting that the pope never said such a thing.

With the atmosphere now politicized and contentious, Sheikh Tamimi rose to speak. He seemed to speak extemporaneously, without reference to a written text, as he delivered a lengthy tirade in Arabic, scoring political points against Israel and earning the applause of the Palestinians present. The pope sat on the stage with his head in his hands while this belligerent speech was delivered. The moderator for this event, Rabbi Dr. Alon Goshen-Gottstein, tried to restore a sense of decorum and mutual respect by imploring people not to use that interreligious forum for partisan polemics. When John Paul II had his turn to speak, he read his prepared speech calling for harmony and cooperation among the three Abrahamic faith communities. In referring to the Holy City, he declared:

> For all of us Jerusalem, as its name indicates, is the "City of Peace." Perhaps no other place in the world communicates the sense of transcendence and divine election that we perceive in her stones and monuments, and in the witness of the three religions living side by side within her walls. Not everything has been or will be easy in this coexistence. But we must find in our respective religious traditions the wisdom and the superior motivation to ensure the triumph of mutual understanding and cordial respect.[12]

The pope went on to invoke the Golden Rule as a common moral standard. But he urged his listeners to go beyond that guideline to embrace "true love of neighbor," which is "based on the conviction that when we love our neighbor we are showing love for God, and when we hurt our neighbor we offend God." Looking back at history, he said:

> We are all aware of past misunderstandings and conflicts, and these still weigh heavily on relationships

---

12. Full speech here at pages 102–6.

between Jews, Christians, and Muslims. We must do all
we can to turn awareness of past offenses and sins into
a firm resolve to build a new future in which there will
be nothing but respectful and fruitful cooperation
between us. The Catholic Church wishes to pursue a
sincere and fruitful interreligious dialogue with the
members of the Jewish faith and the followers of Islam.
Such a dialogue is not an attempt to impose our views
upon others. What it demands of all of us is that, holding to what we believe, we listen respectfully to one
another, seek to discern all that is good and holy in each
other's teachings, and cooperate in supporting everything that favors mutual understanding and peace.

The Jewish, Christian, and Muslim children and
young people present here are a sign of hope and an
incentive for us. Each new generation is a divine gift to
the world. If we pass on to them all that is noble and
good in our traditions, they will make it blossom in
more intense brotherhood and cooperation.

As the pope was uttering these inspiring words, the
two youth choirs that were scheduled to sing together at
the end of the program were locked in heated arguments
in another room, stimulated by the politically oriented
remarks of Rabbi Lau and Sheikh Tamimi. In fact, these
teenagers only agreed to perform their choral piece on
condition that their conductor say, publicly, how distressed
they were by the conduct of the two religious leaders. By
this time, Sheikh Tamimi had left the stage altogether,
leaving the pope and the rabbi and an empty chair.

This event left a sour taste in the mouths of everyone
present. Dr. Goshen-Gottstein, who directs the Jerusalem-

based Elijah School for the Study of Wisdom in World Religions, drew this lesson from the experience: "In instances where religious personalities are involved in politically sensitive situations, events need to be more tightly controlled and orchestrated." In assessing the overall impact of the pope's visit, he said that it produced a positive change in many Israelis' view of Christianity, especially the nonobservant Jewish majority. Most of the Orthodox Jewish community in Israel simply ignored the visit and excluded themselves from it.

The Notre Dame event reminded us that the ongoing political conflict between Israelis and Palestinians pollutes our spiritualities as Jews, Christians, and Muslims. This was true in 2000 and is even more the case today, as we all suffer the consequences of the horrific violence, death, and destruction that erupted just six months following the pope's Jubilee pilgrimage. During his Holy Land visit, the pope did his best to appear politically even-handed as an apostle of peace and justice. His appearances in Bethlehem and the nearby Dheisheh refugee camp signaled his solidarity with the suffering and the aspirations of Palestinians. All along his route, both sides tried to enlist the pontiff as a champion of their own cause, but he resisted the temptation to take sides. He kept to his self-defined mission, moving about the land and offering its wounded inhabitants the balm of indiscriminate love.

There have been a few encouraging signs of interfaith cooperation since his visit, including the Alexandria Declaration issued in January 2002 by Jewish, Christian, and Muslim clerical leaders from Israel, Palestine, and Egypt, as well as the behind-the-scenes negotiations to resolve the forty day siege of the Church of the Nativity in Bethlehem in April–May of 2002. But so much more needs to be done by religious leaders and grassroots activists from the various faith communities, to help create a climate more conducive to political discussions between the two peoples.[13] In this context, where the primary antagonists are Jews and Muslims, Christians can and should act as mediating, reconciling agents of peace with justice. John Paul II demonstrated by his example in March 2000 that such a task is possible and beneficial to all, even if there is deeply ingrained hostility and resistance to change on all sides.

In assessing the impact of the pope's visit, the editor of the *Ha'aretz* daily newspaper said: "Mercy has come to the State of Israel this week and has left banal politics to one side." Avraham Burg, then Speaker of the Knesset (the Israeli parliament), wrote an article for the newspaper *Ma'ariv* in which he described how Israeli Jews were now developing a new understanding of Christianity. What had been viewed as "a religion that spilt blood with the Crusades and the Inquisition has become a religion in which its priests are raised to the level of Righteous among the Nations. It is not possible to understand the fall of totalitarian regimes in Latin America, in South

---

13. See my research report *Healing the Holy Land: Interreligious Peacebuilding in Israel/Palestine*, Peaceworks #51 (Washington, DC: United States Institute of Peace, 2003).

Africa, and in Poland without thinking, in recognition, of the man who yesterday kissed the Western Wall." The most widely read paper in Israel, *Yediot Ahronot*, printed a two-page photo of the pope in prayer before the Wall. Prime Minister Barak told the newspaper, "This historic visit has brought respect for Israel and contributed to *shalom* between Judaism and Christianity."[14]

Four years later, we are trapped in an ongoing political impasse, with its attendant horrors and hardships for both Israelis and Palestinians. The pope still offers prayers for peace from Rome, and religious personalities around the world issue pleas for safeguarding the sanctity of human life and upholding the dignity of every human being.

The political toxicity threatens to overwhelm the spiritual dimension of our lives, in the Holy Land and, after September 11, 2001, everywhere else.

In the midst of political hostility and uncertainty, the relations between the government of Israel and the Christian communities of the land have turned sour during the course of 2003 and 2004. On April 7, 2004, a letter was sent to Israel's ambassador to the United States, Daniel Ayalon, cosigned by the Most Reverend John H. Ricard, SSJ, Bishop of Pensacola-Tallahasee, Florida, and Chairman of the International Policy Committee of the Conference of Catholic Bishops, and by Cardinal William

---

14. All three newspaper quotes reported in "Israeli Press Moved Day After Pope's Farewell," ZENIT.org, dated March 27, 2000, at http://www.zenit.org/english/archive/0003/ZE000327.html#item3.

Keeler, Archbishop of Baltimore and Episcopal Moderator for Catholic-Jewish Relations. After referring to the holy festivals of Passover and Easter which overlapped again this year, and to the joy of the U.S. Catholic community in its experience of dialogue with the Jewish people, the two Catholic officials appealed to Ambassador Ayalon to help rectify some festering problems:

> Against the background of this mutual affection, and in the light of the progress made in Catholic-Jewish relations and honest dialogue these past forty years, we are dismayed at the deterioration of relations between your government and the Catholic Church in Israel and the territories under Israel's control. The growing problem of the denial of visas [for church workers and clerics] or indefinite delay in their issuance, the recent cases of mistreatment of clergy and religious awaiting visa renewal, difficulties over taxation, including those of our own Catholic Relief Services, and the suspension of negotiations on treaties regarding fiscal matters and other issues have created the most difficult situation in living memory for the Church in the Holy Land.
>
> In December, 1993, we celebrated, with your predecessor, the signing of the Fundamental Agreement [between the Holy See and the government of Israel], which is so important, not just for the Church and the government of Israel, but for freedom and pluralism within Israeli society as a whole. Regrettably, as the agreement's tenth anniversary passed, provisions respecting the Church's right to deploy its own personnel in Israel and for both parties to avoid "actions incompatible" with negotiating an agreement on fiscal matters, including taxation, were being routinely

ignored. Despite repeated promises of remedies, the visa problem has grown still more serious, and, the requests of the Holy See notwithstanding, negotiations on a fiscal agreement have been suspended.

With all our affection for the Jewish people and without wavering in our commitment to the state of Israel, the many disappointments and the multiplication of problems are a cause of grave concern.[15]

Another letter was sent on April 13, 2004, this time to President George Bush from the Most Reverend Wilton D. Gregory, President of the U.S. Conference of Catholic Bishops. Bishop Gregory called on the president to be more active in mediating a two-state political accommodation between Israelis and Palestinians. He cited Pope John Paul II's appeal to all parties in the Middle East conflict to "renew dialogue without delay," with the help of "the international community [which] cannot flee from its responsibilities...but must assume them courageously." Also in his letter, Bishop Gregory shared his "grave concern about the deteriorating relations between the Israeli government and the Catholic Church in the Holy Land," identifying the same problems specified in the letter to Ambassador Ayalon.[16]

It is clear from these two letters that the inspiration and promise in the pope's Jubilee pilgrimage are being challenged by new obstacles to improved relations. Jews

---

15. Full letter is on the USCCB's web site at http://www.nccbuscc.org/sdwp/international/ayalon2.htm.

16. Posted on the USCCB web site at http://www.usccb.org/sdwp/international/bush404.htm.

and Catholics must join together to guarantee that our bonds of fraternal affection, nurtured by gestures of repentance and forgiveness, are not undermined by reactionary attitudes. Good will must be continually fostered, and honest dialogue on difficult issues must be facilitated by people who are sensitive to the apprehensions and concerns of all parties.

I hope and pray that the present difficulties can be overcome. Against the backdrop of history, they should be seen as temporary setbacks on a long and uphill path toward a blessed future. Just one hundred years ago, in 1904, a historic encounter took place between Theodore Herzl, the father of modern political Zionism, and Pope Pius X. Herzl went to the Vatican shortly before his death to secure the pope's endorsement of his movement's aim to reestablish Jewish sovereignty in the Holy Land. In his diary, Herzl recorded Pope Pius's response:

> The Jews have not recognized our Lord; therefore we cannot recognize the Jewish people....We cannot prevent the Jews from going to Jerusalem, but we could never sanction it. If you come to Palestine and settle your people there, our churches and priests will be ready to baptize all of you.[17]

It took another sixty years, and the genocide of European Jewry, for this normative Catholic understand-

---

17. Quoted in Sergio I. Minerbi, *The Vatican and Zionism: Conflict in the Holy Land* 1895–1925 (New York: Oxford Univerisity Press, 1990), 100–101. Cf. McGarry's use of the same quote herein, p. 12, footnote #13.

ing to be replaced by "Christian charity" toward Jews on the theological level, divorced from international politics. It took yet another twenty-nine years until the Holy See, under Pope John Paul II's direction, established diplomatic relations with the State of Israel, thereby repudiating Pius X's anti-Zionist theology. And it was not until the media spectacular of John Paul II's Jubilee Pilgrimage that the Church's conditioned resistance to Jewish statehood was finally and unequivocally relegated to the history books.

It is now up to us, all Jews and Catholics who care about redeeming the past and ensuring a blessed future for the coming generations, to add our contributions to the betterment of relations between us. As an unforgettable milestone along this sacred path, Pope John Paul II's Jubilee Pilgrimage to the Holy Land will stand out as a beacon of light to illumine our way.